D0324379

Still Waters

BY W. Phillip Keller

Africa's Wild Glory
Canada's Wild Glory
Splendour From the Land
Splendour From the Sea
Under Wilderness Skies
Under Desert Skies
As a Tree Grows
Bold Under God—Charles Bowen
A Shepherd Looks at Psalm 23
A Layman Looks at the Lord's Prayer
Rabboni . . . Which Is to Say, Master
*A Shepherd Looks at the Good Shepherd and His
   Sheep*
Taming Tension
Expendable
Mountain Splendor
Mighty Man of Valor
A Gardener Looks at the Fruits of the Spirit
Still Waters
Ocean Glory

Still Waters

W. Phillip Keller

Fleming H. Revell Company
Old Tappan, New Jersey

Scripture quotation identified KJV is from the King James Version of the Bible.

Scripture quotation identified LB is from The Living Bible, Copyright © 1971 by Tyndale House Publishers, Wheaton, Illinois 60187. All rights reserved.

Library of Congress Cataloging in Publication Data

Keller, Weldon Phillip
  Still waters.

  1. Keller, Weldon Phillip   2. Country life—British Columbia.   3. British Columbia—Biography
I. Title.
F1088.K447   971.1′04   79-20757
ISBN 0-8007-1092-4

Copyright © 1980 by W. Phillip Keller
Published by Fleming H. Revell Company
All rights reserved
Printed in the United States of America

TO

our little mountain lake

Contents

Preface

Almost exactly ten years have elapsed since I picked up a pen and started to write again after the great loss of my first wife, Phyllis. That was an unsure and trembling start. In fact, then I often wondered if, in truth, I could complete another book.

But the intervening ten years have seen not just one book, but ten, come into full flowering. Some of these have gone on to become national and international best-sellers under our Father's good hand.

Ursula, my second wife and courageous little companion, has shared wholeheartedly in these endeavors. To her I express my hearty gratitude. It has not all been an easy road. Writing is a tremendously demanding discipline. It carries with it discouraging disappointments, as well as deep delights.

From time to time it is imperative that an author should pause to rest, to sharpen his skills, to hone the tools of his trade. To do this requires something that may differ slightly or radically from the form of work he may employ most of the time.

It is akin to the veteran woodsman who is wise enough to stop and rest from his chopping and sawing. He will perch up on a stump, take a file from his pocket to touch up the teeth of his saw, draw out a whetstone to hone the edge of his axe razor sharp. Then, refreshed and restored, he will return to work doubly equipped.

Still Waters has been just such an interlude; it has been a labor of love. Time was set aside to record this interlude for the sheer joy of writing. The theme is one that has enriched my own spirit.

My most earnest hope is that it might in some significant way inspire and enrich the reader.

W. PHILLIP KELLER

One

The Search for "Still Waters"

Those who have read some of my previous books, such as *Canada's Wild Glory*, *Splendour From the Land*, *Under Desert Skies* and *A Shepherd Looks at Psalm 23*, will know that I am a man with an intense, unrelenting love for the land. But beyond this basic, fundamental fondness for earth and trees, plants, shrubs, grass and livestock, the whole out-of-doors is essentially my home territory. It is there I feel a unique oneness with all things wild and free.

A number of my books have dealt with this dimension of life. *Africa's Wild Glory*, *Under Wilderness Skies*, *Travels of the Tortoise* and *Mountain Splendor* have all endeavored to share with the reader some of the powerful impulses and deep delights that have made my life in the outdoors such an incredible adventure. They have recounted some of the exciting experiences of living close to the land. They have revealed those values and ideals that are essential for the preservation of wild places and wildlife, which are an integral part of our wholeness as a society.

For several years my work and responsibilities made it imperative for me to live in the city. True, it was not a large metropolis, but it was still an urban environment. My wife and I rented a spacious suite in a modern high-rise building. We were fortunate to find one with pleasant views across the valley and within easy walking distance of the lake. Had it not been for the opportunities to slip away quietly for long tramps along the beach, my stay in the city would have been much more painful than it was.

In the apartment, I tasted the sort of life that is the lot of millions upon millions of city residents. We enjoyed all the conveniences and comforts associated with a man-made environment. There were thermostats and double-glass windows and electric doors and wall-to-wall carpeting and air conditioning to control the indoor climate.

There were double bathrooms, gleaming with tile and chrome fixtures. Built-in appliances such as oven, dishwasher, stove, refrigerator, washer and drier all made for the most modern mode of existence. Two telephones one beside the bed, kept us in immediate contact with the entire city and all of its busy life. Underground security parking, electric doors, elevators and paved drives insured that we were sheltered from the elements of wind, snow, sleet or rain.

Yet, amid all this apparent affluence and seeming security, a strange sensation of insecurity hovered in the background. There was a profound, pervading promise of vulnerability to our pretty place. Fortunately we were reluctant to purchase property of this sort; rather we rented. This at least reduced the risks of becoming enmeshed and terribly trapped in an unwholesome environment.

The word *unwholesome* was chosen with great care, for I never felt completely at ease in this artificial, urban environment. In a sense I felt caged in. I was cramped and constricted by my surroundings of steel, stucco, concrete and asphalt. They tended to cut me off from contact—intimate contact—with the earth. My feet were always insulated from the touch of soil and grass and leaves and twigs and sand and rock. My face craved the kiss of the sun, the caress of the wind or the stimulation of snow and rain. The air I breathed was stale, often charged with fumes of carbon monoxide or industrial wastes. The water I drank came through the pipes so contaminated with chlorine it was scarcely potable, much less palatable to one who has drunk deeply from mountain streams. Most of the food I ate was procured from the supermarket, its origin often thousands of miles away in some foreign land.

Somehow I sensed that my dependence upon others to supply me with power, light, heat, water, food and shelter from afar made me very vulnerable. One lightning strike or one labor strike, and my artificial, man-made world could imprison me helplessly in the midst of modern devices.

Because of all this, a deep subconscious unease often lay upon my spirit. My wife, Cheri (her pet name), and I would sometimes speak of this deep disquiet in our more somber moments. She, as a young girl, had gone through the agony and anguish of a great war in Europe. She knew firsthand what it was to be cut off by catastrophe from the elemental resources of the land. She had stood in line for hours, shivering in the cold, waiting for a meager handout of bread or milk or meat. She had felt the awesome, gnawing hunger pangs of unsatisfied appetite. She had been sent on errands to the countryside, to exchange the finest of laces and linens for a sack of potatoes or a pound of butter.

Beyond all of these vague, yet sinister, aspects of our vulnerability lay the very tangible and tough realities of day-to-day living. Because of inflation; because of increased labor costs; because of the accelerating energy crisis; because of international monetary exchanges, the bills we had to pay from month to month kept going up and up. Charges for power, heat, light, food, water, telephone and transportation escalated steadily.

I am too free a spirit to be trapped by the tensions of my times. And, as we contemplated a change, I decided that we would search for some still waters, where the tyranny of twentieth-century urban life would not intrude. We would look for a spot somewhat removed from the noise and confusion of city living. It would not be easy to find. Privacy, seclusion and peace are rapidly becoming the rarest commodities in a crowded world. The place where a person could still, at least to a degree, derive his life and sustenance from his immediate surroundings by his own strength was not easy to stumble across.

But we would try.

I wanted to get back to basics.

There was a longing to re-establish contact with the land. Again I would draw my sustenance and comfort directly from the resources of the earth around me. With the strength of my body and keen awareness of my mind, I wanted to sense and know what it was to be a free and independent man, moving in gentle harmony with the outdoor seasons and natural environment that supported me.

This quest for a quiet life was more than just a move from the city to the country. It involved more than merely relocating ourselves geographically in a rural setting.

It was also an inner readjustment.

There was also a deep inner hunger, a fierce longing, for stillness and silence and serenity. I needed space for my soul to rest from the rush and clamor of city tensions.

One of civilization's most formidable forces, which had exacted an enormous toll of tension from me, was traffic noise. The unrelenting roar of trucks, screech of cars and staccato gunfire of motorbikes gunning up the hill past our place made many nights a nightmare. The drone of city traffic, power mowers, powerboats, power street sweepers and air traffic overhead beat upon our eardrums all day long.

Even though subconsciously I endeavored to shut out this intrusion, the noise pollution preyed upon me. It generated a revulsion in my inner being, which resented the racket that beat about me with such remorseless intensity. Sigurd Olson expressed this exasperation very pointedly in his book *Singing Wilderness:*

> More and more do we realize that quiet is impor-
> tant to our happiness. In our cities the constant beat
> of strange and foreign wave lengths on our primal
> senses beats us into neuroticism, changes us from
> creatures who once knew the silences to fretful, un-
> certain beings immersed in a cacophony of noise
> which destroys sanity and equilibrium.

But beyond all these considerations, the search for still waters was in a sense a search for spiritual refreshment: to be still and know God; to sense His presence; to commune with Him quietly, without undue haste or rush.

Just to sit softly in the twilight beside a lake or on a bluff of rock in some quiet glade and be glad He, too, was there sharing the setting with me; this I sought.

There are those who will claim that to try and go back to our beginnings is to live life in reverse. They assert vehemently that we cannot turn back the clock and re-duce the tempo of our times.

Perhaps for the vast multitudes born and cradled in the complexity of great cities, this is true. Perhaps from the hour of their conception they have been subtly con-ditioned, even in their mothers' warm wombs, to the world of stress and strain around them. But for me, this was not so. I was born and reared in the great, open, sweeping expanses of Africa's plains and bush. I am a product of the wilds, a son of the wilderness. Wide vis-tas, open spaces, long views, the warm sun, vagrant winds and star-filled nights in untamed country are the fabric fashioned into my rough character. It was upon these that my boyhood soul was built into manhood. And if long removed from them, even as a man in his twilight years, I ached for them with profound pain.

No, indeed, finding still waters in our busy, boisterous, twentieth century would not be easy.

For it was also a search for simplicity. It was a quest for basic human self-reliance.

I was deliberately turning my back upon the easy life of reliance on others to meet my needs. With the output of my own strength, the use of my own wits, the exertion of my own muscles, I would seek independence amid a pathetically dependent society.

In so far as it was possible and practical, I wanted to dig my own garden, grow much of my own food, gather my own fuel and nourish my own soul with the natural beauties about me. I wanted to live in serenity and in dignity. For me, peace of mind, stillness of spirit and soundness of health were more important than any prestige or prominence that hectic city life might proffer.

The mute question was, could such a way of life be rediscovered? Could it be grasped again by a man well advanced in years? Could it be tasted and relished, even if only briefly, before that last call came to go home where change and decay no longer dismay?

Two
The Find

To find the sort of spot we dreamed about would not be easy. Twenty-five years ago it would have been much, much easier. But with the passing of time, most of the desirable properties had been taken up and developed to a high degree.

There had been many years of prosperity, affluence and rapid urban growth. Investors had large sums to spend on real estate. Land values soared to unheard-of heights, and many wealthy families were looking for some quiet corner in the country where they could have a second home. These rural retreats were often little more than status symbols. To own a summer house in the hills or beside a lake was to parade one's prosperity, just as owning a second car was at one time a mark of financial success.

In spite of the enormous competition, we set out in earnest to see what was available. In the usual manner, we followed the newspaper advertisements, watched For Sale signs along the roads, allowed agents to drag us from place to place, trying to persuade us to buy something not really suited to our needs. But we were not to be diverted or dissuaded from our dream. I refused to buy something not suited to us.

It was a discouraging search. So many times we seemed to be hot on the trail of a tempting spot, only to discover that it had enormous disadvantages or drawbacks. Sometimes properties were blatantly misrepresented. The advertisement would sound so appealing, but the place itself would turn out to be appalling.

Then, one gentle spring day, I returned to a little lakeside cottage that had been given only a cursory glance several months before. It looked rather dilapidated, and the original asking price had been outrageous. But suddenly, because of illness, the owner had been compelled to sell, and now the value asked had been substantially reduced, to a more reasonable level.

The morning I went to take a second look, I discovered that the adjoining land was also for sale. Together, the two properties would provide the sort of privacy and seclusion that we sought. But I was still not sure the cottage was capable of accommodating us comfortably. It looked to be not much more than a thin shell of a structure, suited to a few fleeting summer weeks. The question was, could it be converted into a reasonably suitable permanent residence? We would have to look inside.

The location left something to be desired. It was down a short dead-end road, rather too close to a main arterial road to suit my taste. Fortunately, a thick screen of assorted trees and native shrubs surrounded the place. The cottage, when the leaves were out, could not be seen from the main highway. It sat tucked away on a little shelf of sward beside the lake, unknown and unnoticed by most of those who drove past.

To a degree, this was not altogether undesirable. At least we were convenient to an all-weather road. There would be no need to fight sleet and ice and deep drifts of winter snow to get in and out during adverse weather. I had endured more than my share of such roads in previous places I had owned across the years.

Second, even though I sought a place of peace and quiet for writing, I did not wish to become totally detached from the tempo of my times. Too many authors and thinkers and scholars ensconce themselves in ivory-tower isolation. They lose touch with the tough realities of their generation. For me, the muffled rumble and roar of traffic that filtered down through the trees would be a constant, solemn reminder of the stern, competitive, noisy, high-speed world in which I live.

To a degree, depending upon the atmospheric conditions and direction of the wind, the sounds of speeding vehicles would rise or diminish. Sometimes they were so muted they could scarcely be heard. On other occasions their noise seemed to be unduly amplified by the lake surface or the towering cliffs behind. Yet seldom were the lap of water or rustle of leaves inaudible.

On the whole, despite the proximity of the paved highway, peace and tranquility prevailed in this gentle spot. Sufficiently so that as I strolled around its untidy and rather neglected grounds, I could clearly hear the spring songs of the western meadowlarks nesting in the sagebrush hills above us. I could also hear the clear, piercing, plaintive notes of a loon on the lake. They were sounds that surmounted all those other sounds and spoke peace to my spirit.

Down at the water's edge, there was the soft lap of water on stones—the lazy lullaby of the lake washing back and forth on the rocks in front of the cottage. It was an intimate, satisfying sensation to sit there watching the wind-stirred riffles run up to my feet, yet seldom break the satin-smooth surface of the water.

Between breezes, the lake would lie perfectly still. It was cupped in a warm valley between gaunt, gnarled ridges of rock and shale. Their bold battlements of brown and gray formations were mirrored in the still waters with immaculate, flawless perfection.

I had never been on a property that seemed to have such an intimate interaction with a body of water. Most homes and houses built on beaches or shorelines stand back a bit from the water's edge. It is as if they stand there as onlookers at a respectable distance. They enjoy the view, but prefer not to come too close.

Here it was totally different. The lake almost embraced the cottage on two sides. It sang on the tiny sand beach only a few feet from the door. It rippled in the reeds that ran along the edge of the grass glades. Sunlight glancing off its surface flooded the great glass windows facing it. The presence of the lake itself was astonishingly pervasive. It was everywhere around, moving and breathing. It was an environment that was relatively new and exciting to one, like myself, who had never lived in such close association with a mountain lake.

I felt inexorably drawn under its spell. Quickly I began to discover that this could be a stimulating spot to live. I had read that lakes were too placid, too serene, too quiet to stimulate a writer, but a few hours beside this body of water convinced me otherwise. Here one was in immediate contact with a whole web of life that was in constant motion. Its many moods, its changing seasons, its abundant bird life, its varied habitats suited to all sorts of animals, made it a miniature world of endless delight and wonder.

I stumbled across several stubs of poplar that still bore the chiseled tooth marks of beavers. As I scrambled along the shore, a beautiful dark mink darted along a log. On the path behind the cottage, a coyote had left his droppings in the gravel. At night his wilderness cry would echo across the lake from the brown bluffs above us.

I found an open glade, cleared from the woods that flourished along the shore. Its soil was dark, rich, mellow with the accumulated leaf mold of uncounted centuries. It had been carved from the wilderness by some sturdy pioneer long since forgotten. With sweat and skill and the labor of love, it could be made into a bountiful garden for fruit and vegetables.

The longer I looked around, the more convinced I was that at last we had found our spot. It was wild enough, untamed enough, to appeal to my wilderness spirit. A black bear had been seen swimming across the lake a few days before. The wild bighorn sheep were lambing on the rock bluffs overlooking the cottage. And across the lake, bands of mule deer came down at dawn to drink, their shining coats reflected in the still waters.

But the cottage itself remained a question. A few days later we were shown inside. To our unbounded surprise and delight, it was far, far better than its weathered exterior had indicated.

It was of sturdy open-beam construction. It was not a shack at all, but an all-cedar cottage, with great expanses of glass opening onto the lake. An atmosphere of spaciousness, warmth and charm came from the softwood interior. The native cedar shone satin smooth and gave off the rich aroma of forest fragrance.

Cheri and I looked at each other. A knowing look of mutual approval and agreement passed between us. *This was it. We had found it. The search was over!* No words were spoken, but these were the sentiments of our spirits, sure and certain.

The previous occupants had been temporary tenants, and, as is always the case, the cottage showed signs of neglect and carelessness. It would take time and work to restore its luster. Minor interior alterations would have to be made to suit our life-style. There were no proper clothes cupboards. Heating arrangements were inadequate for winter weather. Floor coverings would have to be replaced. Insulation of the roof and walls would have to be undertaken.

None of these were unduly difficult. By fall, when the great black birches turned their greenery into flaming gold, the little cottage would be a snug home, sheathed and sealed against winter storms.

Sitting on the open sun deck in the gentle spring sunshine, we wrote out an offer to purchase the property. In a few days it would be ours. It was the opening of a brand-new chapter in our lives. We had no idea just how rich and full and exciting its pages would be. It was another step of adventure on the trail of a life already replete with great satisfactions and enormous thrills.

In a very genuine and sincere sense, we knew it was the place of our heavenly Father's arrangement for us. Often we had turned to Him, seeking definite direction in our decisions. It is far too easy to stumble into traps when purchasing property. He had been our senior counselor and consultant. The clear guidance He gave brought us to something better than we had ever imagined.

One of our deep desires was that this spot should be not just an inspiration to us, but to all others who visited us, who had a chance to taste its tranquility.

Standing beneath the birches, looking across the shining loveliness of the lake, its name came to me clearly: "We will call it 'Still Waters,' " for it is our Lord who led us here."

Three
The Fireplace

Because "Still Waters" in its original state was basically only a summer cabin, it lacked any proper heating arrangement for winter weather. There was a small fireplace that would take the chill off a cool June evening, but it was far from adequate to face the fury of a fierce northerly in November.

It was obvious something much more substantial would have to be provided to pour heat into the place at a steady pace, no matter how ruthless the storms were that raged around our rough walls.

Since the energy crisis has crept up on our contemporary world, hundreds of thousands of home owners have turned back to wood and coal in search of fuel savings. A

whole new generation of efficient wood- and coal-
burning stoves, heaters and fireplaces has found a ready
market among embattled people aroused by ever-
increasing fuel costs.

So I went in search of some sort of fireplace unit,
heater or stove that would serve several purposes at once
with a maximum of efficiency. It was nearly as difficult as
deciding on a new car. There are a multitude of models,
designs and makes to choose from. They are pro-
moted and advertised with beautiful literature and be-
guiling brochures. But to find the type best suited to our
needs meant more than just looking at lovely pictures
put out by the manufacturers.

After reading all we could and tramping through all
the stores, I came across the unit that impressed me the
most. It was simple in design, yet elegant in appearance.
Made of heavy, quarter-inch steel, fully lined with heavy
firebrick, it could serve as a cook stove, heater or open
fireplace.

But the price seemed prohibitive.

Though only one unit remained for sale, I procrasti-
nated about purchasing it. Finally the decision could not
be deferred any longer. That day I quietly bowed my
head and requested supernatural guidance from God,
my Father, in proceeding to purchase it.

When I asked to be shown the unit, I was taken out to
the warehouse by a young man from the company whom
I had not met before. He quickly assured me this particular model was the finest and only trouble-free unit they
had ever stocked. This helped to harden my resolve.

Then, almost in the same breath, he went on to inform
me that he was the son of the owner of the company. It

was his special privilege to extend a discount to any customer. He would be glad to knock off 10 percent then and there, if I would take it off his hands. Would I! My heart leaped with gratitude, the sale was consummated and I walked out of the store breathing deeply, "Thank You, Father!"

The little heater, not even three feet high or wide, weighed nearly a quarter of a ton. It was not the sort of thing one just picks up or pushes around at will. It was a piece of equipment you quickly learned to respect.

A kind friend came over to help move it inside, but the two of us could hardly budge it, so we called upon our wives to help us. Heaving, straining, shoving and pushing, we finally got it into place. It was terribly tricky, fitting the smoke pipes just right. I had measured their length to the exact fraction of an inch. But by tipping the stove gently on one side, we were able to insert them at an angle, and then slide the unit into place. All of us were puffing and heaving with the exertion, but the heater stood square and straight and sure in its place when we were through.

It turned out to be one of those pieces of equipment that work to perfection. In fact, it so far surpassed our expectations that we still marvel at its efficiency and rave to our friends about its performance.

Adorning its black bulk are beautiful, gleaming, stainless-steel knobs. Its name, too, is emblazoned in bold shining silver across the front. The fire screen used when an open fire is desired is also fabricated from glowing stainless steel, so that the entire unit stands as a handsome piece to enhance our home.

I had a friend, who is a skilled tinsmith, construct a

metal tray in which the stove would stand. This I filled
with glacial stones and rocks from the hills above us.
Each stone was selected with loving care for its sparkle,
color and shape. These were each washed carefully in
the lake, then arranged around the base in a beautiful,
natural mosaic of mountain rocks.

Behind the fireplace, to protect the wooden walls from
its heat, I decided to place a single rugged slab of granite. A friend and I went to the edge of a gaunt canyon
back of our cottage. There an outcrop of beautiful rock
had split into sheets of stone that could be pried off the
basement formations. With enormous care, I picked out a
piece that I felt would exactly suit the cottage.

It was no easy thing to carry this giant slab of stone out
of the hills. We made a crude cradle of poles and ropes to
carry it. Then, stumbling along a few steps at a time, we
slowly struggled up the canyon trail.

Now the rock stands serenely back of the heater,
adorned with patches of lovely lichens and bits of moss
that remind us of the rugged hills from whence it came.

Because of the basic design of the heater, which uses a
steel baffle, it burns a minimum of fuel with a maximum
of heat. In ten minutes time, even a moderate fire begins
to warm the entire cottage. Once the heavy steel unit,
along with the giant slab of granite behind it, are hot,
they remain so for hours, permeating the whole place
with that gentle, living, vibrant heat that is so uniquely
characteristic of wood fuel. Its aroma fills our home, and
the fragrance of the fire lends an ancient aura of goodwill
and good cheer to the atmosphere.

When I come back to the cottage—whether from working in the garden, hiking in the hills or canoeing across

the lake—I am welcomed by the pungent perfume of wood smoke. There is something warm and wonderful in its enchantment, akin to being greeted at the door by the open arms and warm embrace of a loving woman.

We spend hours and hours of quiet contentment beside this fireplace. Its flames dance up the chimney in bright hues of gold, yellow, red, blue and sometimes even green, when a piece of wood streaked with fungus or lichens is licked by the fire.

The flames flicker and play in reflection on the windowpanes. They play and dance, too, in the eyes and faces of those who sit quietly before them, borne away in daydreams of delight.

Even cutting and gathering wood for this fireplace is no chore. It uses so little and burns so efficiently that my woodpile for the winter was ten times bigger than I needed. Few are the things in life which have so far surpassed our happiest hopes.

Four
Inside "Still Waters"

When we first came to "Still Waters," the cabin itself posed somewhat of a problem. It had been used only for casual summer interludes. Though built of the best native cedar planks, it was still not much more than a mere shell, meant to shelter its occupants from the elements.

Being of open-beam construction, with great expanses of glass overlooking the lake, it was a handsome summer retreat. But the very attributes that worked to its special advantage in warm weather made it equally unsuitable for winter residence. With its single-layer board walls, high open-loft ceilings and giant windows, there was ample air movement and space to moderate summer's scorching heat.

All of this, however, would have to be altered to make it habitable when winter winds hauled down across the lake from the north. Amid snow and ice and driving sub-zero sleet, it would need to be much more snug and tight against the weather.

To accomplish this, we sought the services of a veteran carpenter. With his long experience and great drive, he quickly converted it from a mere cabin to a snug, comfortable cottage. Assisted by his two young and sturdy nephews, he performed a modern miracle in less than a week of work.

First he put on a double roof, fully insulated. This would retain all the heat that formerly escaped upwards and outwards through the single tongue-and-groove cedar roof. Then he double glazed all the giant windows. The glass was put in with meticulous precision, fully sealed and charged with desiccant between the air spaces, to prevent fogging or condensation.

Finally, he insulated all the outside walls and sheathed them again in satin-lustered native cedar. It made for a beautiful weather-tight structure. With painstaking care, he personally selected each piece of cedar that went on the walls.

When the whole transformation was complete, the cottage stood glowing in its natural wood tones. No one would ever suspect that it had been so dramatically altered, since its entire beautiful interior remained untouched, in its native woodsy splendor. Smooth cedar planking, rich with its warm hues of brown, red and bronze, gave the little home an aura of coziness and contentment.

We removed one large set of sliding glass doors that

opened onto the deck. In its place we installed a huge picture window that gives an unobstructed view over the lawns and lake to the rugged hills beyond.

The alterations were done in midsummer, at the hottest time of the desert year. Immediately, we noticed that the modifications improved the liveability of the cottage. Its double roof and walls kept out the blazing heat, and the double glass tempered the burning summer sun. So we had gained dramatically in every direction, much to our delight.

The elderly carpenter and his youthful helpers were excellent craftsmen. They worked with vigor and zest, despite the appalling heat. An occasional plunge in the lake would cool them off. And when the day's work was done, one knew that their time had been spent to the optimum.

The refurbishing of the cottage was a tremendous treat. So often it is common to hear people complain about shoddy workmanship and slipshod labor. But we were given a delectable taste of old-fashioned craftsmanship at its best. A certain pride of accomplishment and inherent skill in workmanship had been apparent in the whole project. When the men were done, we were left with the distinct impression that this had been a labor of love.

Inside the cottage, a pronounced atmosphere of peace and serenity prevails. There is something distinctly warm and woodsy about it. It blends beautifully with the birches and boulders and beaches around it. It is almost as if part of the outdoors has been brought indoors. One blends with the other. The inside is not separated from the outside by superficial barriers. Looking in is as much

an extension of one's view as looking out is a widening of
one's vision.

On the wooden walls there hang gorgeous genuine oil
paintings of mountain scenes and native wildlife. These
have come into our care through the unique artistry of
my friend Karl Wood. Acclaimed and recognized as one
of Canada's foremost mountain painters, his exquisite
work lends an atmosphere of authentic mountain grandeur to our cottage.

There are other unique furnishings, too, which are essentially a part of our native upland world of forests, lake
and hills. A beautiful wood-burl table, fashioned from a
giant Douglas fir and mounted on elk antlers, graces the
living room. The antlers were a pair of crown-royals that
I picked up on a remote ridge in the northern Rockies on
my first expedition into that rugged wilderness.

On my desk stands a handsome lamp. Its base is a rich,
dark-red slab of native juniper, its pedestal a twisted
greasewood stem. And adorning it are a pair of California
quail: a cock and hen beautifully posed.

From the open-beamed ceiling hangs a cheerful chandelier created from two sets of dainty whitetail-deer
antlers. Often we look across the lake and watch these
deer feeding at the water's edge. Now several sets of
their cast-off crowns grace our home, flooding it with
charm and good cheer.

Here and there on the walls there are other mounted
birds. A gorgeous golden-breasted meadowlark, singing
his heart out, reminds us of our songsters on the sagebrush benches above us. The waxwing is one of hundreds that come winging through the valley to gorge
themselves on wild-rose hips and mountain-ash berries.

All these mounts have been prepared and fashioned by my friend Abe Braun. Though now semiretired, he is among the finest taxidermists on the continent. His superb workmanship is found from the Yukon to Panama. For our part, we feel honored to have a few pieces of his superb craftsmanship in our care. It lends enormous atmosphere to our home.

We are people who find deep pleasure in common things: a twisted piece of driftwood; a gnarled, wave-washed root; a slab of stone, shattered and shining with minerals; a spray of maple leaves, scarlet and gold; sprigs of pine and fir, redolent with resin and the fragrance of the forest; bouquets of wild desert flowers gathered from the hills; a gnarled piece of beaver wood, cut by chisel-sharp teeth; giant ponderosa pinecones and dainty spruce cones.

These are all a part of the wild world in which we live and work and play. They are the warp and woof of our mountain realm. We relish them, revel in them, then happily pass them on to friends or visitors.

Inherently there is something very sure and very satisfying in these common bonds between the earth and us. We sense and know instinctively that we are not separated from the source of our sustenance and inspiration by man-made barriers. Here there is an intimacy with the earth that sustains us, the environment that supports us, the surroundings that inspire us and set our spirits singing.

Inside "Still Waters," there is a profound awareness of belonging—in a primitive, pristine way—to the world around us. Even the manner in which the cottage snuggles into its lakeside setting among the trees and shrubs and rocks and grass lends the feeling of being native to the landscape. It does not impose or intrude upon its surroundings. It is so much at peace in its place that many have passed it by for years, not even knowing it was there, resting quietly among its friendly trees.

This little cottage by the lake is a place of quiet contentment. To those friends and visitors who come within its walls, it speaks serenity. Here is stilled the rush and noise of urban life, and in its place there descends the stillness of nature's gentle ways.

Always, our hope and prayer and desire remain that anyone setting foot within our wooden walls will go away richer than when they came: richer in memories of a few moments of repose, in which they sensed the gentle touch of God's gracious Spirit on their souls.

To help achieve this end, we make sure that music plays a prominent part in our lives. But this *music* of which I speak is not all of the man-made sort.

Many of the melodies played around "Still Waters" are as ancient as our hills, as ageless as our desert stars. This music caressed and cheered this valley centuries before the first Indians set foot upon its hot, sandy benches. It is music that comes drifting in on the breezes through our open windows; it is a medley of songs that soothes our spirits as we step to the open door.

There are the tremulous notes of meadowlarks and orioles, chickadees and song sparrows. There are the haunting, long-drawn cries of the loons on the lake, the coyotes on the cliffs. There is the strident, stirring sound of Canada geese on wing, as well as sandhill cranes and flights of ducks crossing the sky in spectacular flocks.

Added to these are the lap of waves on rock and sand:

the rhythmic splash of water shattering on stone. The rush and gush of white-crested waves, pushed and plowed by the wind at work on the lake, stirs our souls.

That same wind whistles and sings and whoops its way through the trees. The branches bend and bow and billow in the blustery breezes. They brush and rub their leaves together in a symphony of sound that makes sleep come sweetly and the rest refreshing.

We are rich with melodies of a hundred sorts. To these we add the joy of music of our own making. Despite our limited space, a modest organ graces our home. Cheri, in her own winsome ways, was able to purchase the instrument at a fraction of its original price. From it we draw hours of pleasure, playing our favorite songs and hymns.

Added to all this, we can tune into a high-fidelity good-music station. The strains of majestic symphonies and the great classics are received within our warm walls, bringing to them inspiration and uplift for all who are within earshot. And because of all this, we know ourselves to be blessed.

Five
Tree Planting

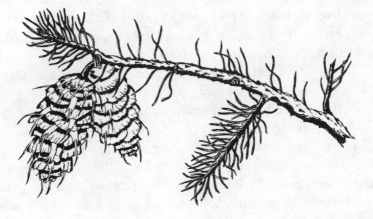

Close behind "Still Waters" runs a busy highway. It
is one of the main north-south travel routes through
our mountain country. Because of the tourist influx
drawn by the sunny skies, beautiful beaches, lovely
lakes, mighty mountains and the bountiful fruit of the
valley, this is a busy, noisy thoroughfare in summer.
The rest of the year, it is less congested and thunder-
ous.

To help screen ourselves from the traffic sounds, it was
decided to plant trees along the road. There were trees
there already, but it seems one can never have too many,
if it is privacy and seclusion that are desired. To a degree, the native poplars, birches and junipers already

41

supplied a leafy screen. But we wanted even more protection.

I decided on planting Lombardy poplars for an avenue of stately, rapidly growing trees. A nearby nursery supplied me with a fine set of sturdy specimens. A friend came to help dig the deep holes. One morning's hard work saw all the slim-shaped trees, still bare of leaves, standing in place, erect and graceful. Digging the holes helped us to discover that our soil was deeper, darker and of better content than I had ever supposed.

There is something sacred about planting trees. There is permanency, hope and a long look down the years ahead in this rite. It is sacramental, in the sense that one is aware the trees may very well be there long after the planter has passed on. Standing in their place beneath the blazing summer sun, bent beneath winter snows, they will grace the landscape long years after I am gone.

There is love and affection and compassion bound up with growing trees. They must be watered and staked and pruned and sprayed, to forestall the adversity of their environment and predators. Beautiful trees take more than just being plunked in place to thrive. So between trees and men there begins to emerge a bond of affection and endearment.

I watched the row of Lombardies with co-mingled awe and delight. In the first summer's growth, they shot up nearly six feet. Great, green, gorgeous leaves unfurled from their swelling buds to flutter like emerald flags, blowing in the breeze. I cut back the most advanced shoots to thicken up the growth, making their dense branches an even better sound barrier.

By late fall, they were a galaxy of gold, each leaf gilded

yellow, flashing back the sunlight that struck its surface. In a few years the avenue would be a landmark in the valley, a sight to gladden the spirit of any passersby.

I also planted some trees of heaven. These are a vigorous, large-leaved tree, with a distinctly tropical appearance. Yet they are tough enough to endure a cold winter. They thrive on marginal land and can endure dire drought. In late summer, their foliage changes to a rich bronze that is arresting in its diversity.

An amusing aspect of this little venture was that the trees came from a friend who had kindly dug them up from a roadside site. He placed them carefully in boxes and then brought them to me. At the time, all the young saplings were stripped and bare of leaves, so I planted each in its special spot with the utmost care.

To my chagrin, in a few weeks, when the little trees leafed out, I discovered that several of my supposed trees of heaven were in fact the dreaded poison oak, a local shrub that thrives in our area of the country. I am very susceptible to poison oak, so these interlopers were soon torn from the soil, though not without a hearty laugh. In their dormant winter condition, they had looked very much like the little tree saplings.

Speaking of poison oak, it is worthy of mention that the finest antidote to its painful blisters is the application of ordinary Crest toothpaste. This is worth remembering, because many of the more expensive remedies provide little or no relief at all.

I also planted a variety of native and exotic junipers, some of which were dug from the hills around us. They are tough, hardy trees with beautiful foliage of various hues and forms. I have always admired these durable, graceful trees, which thrive under semidesert conditions in the toughest terrain. I sometimes layer the lower limbs of special trees in the mountains, in the hope that one day I shall return to retrieve a new sapling started in this simple way.

Maples are also among my favorites. The only native maple that does well in our high country is the hardy little vine maple. In many places, it really is not much more than a multistemmed bush. The largest specimen I ever saw was no more than thirty feet high, with the largest stem about ten inches across. It had been bulldozed out of the ground to make a logging road. I cut it up for the fireplace. Its hard, dense wood gave off heat equal to the best of coal.

I dug up and replanted one of these little maples in our rockery. In fall its foliage will flame from yellow to orange and finally crimson. It will be a thing of glorious beauty against the blue backdrop of the lake.

I also planted a delicate, split-leaved, scarlet Japanese maple. Whether it can withstand the cutting winter winds that whip across the lake to lash its limbs with snow and sleet remains to be seen. Time alone will tell. For one summer, at least, its feathery foliage gave us quiet delight, as it spread itself in the shelter of the black birches.

Because the red sugar maple of the east has always been such a thrilling tree to me, I planted one of these. At first it seemed to suffer with our intense summer heat. It had purposely been placed in a sheltered spot with partial shade, but even there it languished. In October it flamed scarlet, but that may well have been a final farewell salute to an environment too tough to endure.

What we in our western valley may lack in colorful deciduous trees is more than made up for by our fiery native sumac. It thrives on even the driest gravel benches, where otherwise only sagebrush, greasewood and cactus can survive. I planted sumac in strategic places all around "Still Waters." Its luxuriant summer foliage and incandescent autumn colors are sheer joy—a delight to the eye and heart of any outdoorsman.

The last tree planted during our first season was a golden-needled larch from the high hills. Cheri and I made a special trip to the high country, just to pick one out. Tenderly we lifted it from its native ridge and bore it down beside the lake. It stands erect at the water's edge. If all goes well, its feathery form and golden needles will enhance "Still Waters" for a hundred years to come.

Six
Mellow Moods

Perhaps the most pronounced and powerful impact that "Still Waters" made upon my spirit was in providing a sense of peace. Not that its atmosphere was still and static; it was not. But there lingered here an element of repose and harmony not often found in our busy world.

This peace was woven from many strands of the pulsing life about us. It came partly from our natural setting; partly from the other life forms that shared our lakeside world; partly from the kind neighbors and friends who came to call.

Never before had I lived in such close proximity and intimate contact with a mountain lake. Little did I realize its mellow moods would make such an enormous impact upon my soul. It was a moving and uplifting experience to be under its majestic spell.

This was true even when inside the cottage. Its expansive floor-to-ceiling windows gave the sensation that indoors and outdoors were one continuous whole. Often, as we sat at our meals or relaxed in the front room, I had the distinct impression of being one with the trees and shrubs, the lake and the hills that surrounded us. The feeling was one, not of human intrusion, but rather of having ourselves completely accepted and encircled by our natural surroundings.

There is something very special about such a setting. One *belongs,* in a unique and comforting way. And in this quiet acceptance lies great consolation. Put another way, it would be appropriate to say that it was not man who was imposing his dominant will on his surroundings, but rather had allowed himself to be enfolded and fully accepted into the natural community.

We of the highly sophisticated, hard, brittle, plastic Western world seldom sense this oneness with nature. We are too dedicated to material progress; to the use of mechanical power for imposing our will on the world; to speed and haste and great waste.

An African proverb that has comprised a large part of my lifelong philosophy is stated thus: *"Haraka, haraka, hana baraka,"* which in our idiom is, "Haste, haste, but no blessing."

The gentle tempo of the passing seasons at "Still Waters" reinforced this deep conviction. Some of my contemporaries may have raised their eyebrows and shaken their heads in disbelief at our simple life-style in that spot. But, for me, it became a quiet, serene backwater in a busy, boisterous world.

After all, there are certain values in life that money and material wealth can never purchase. Gold and silver, stocks and bonds, bank accounts and investment securities are not sufficient to assure peace of heart or serenity of spirit.

What price can be placed upon a life of simplicity, free from the fret and strain of trying to keep pace in a man-killing society? What will a person give in exchange for the quiet ecstasy of living gently in harmony with the seasons? What consolation can surpass that of the secure inner assurance that this indeed is my Father's world, in which He cares for me with intense personal interest?

At "Still Waters," we were constantly reminded that this caring was not confined or directed only toward us human beings. It embraced and enfolded the whole world around us. The trees and shrubs, with their foliage shining in the sun; the soft, sweet, fragrant grasses and flowers that flourished on our hills; the birds that built their nests and reared their young all around us; the insects that hummed in the sun and flitted across the lake; the wild deer and mountain sheep and mink and beavers and bears whose realm we shared; all reminded us that we were friends and neighbors. As the ancient Indians would say, we were all "brothers beneath the sun."

In this realization, we were back to basic beginnings. We delude ourselves if we believe our Father cares only for human beings. His assurance to us is otherwise. It is He who clothes the flowers of the field in great glory; He knows when a fledgling falls.

Sensations of this sort often engulfed my spirit as day drew to a close. Sitting in the soft afterglow of the setting sun, there were happy, mellow interludes in which to think long thoughts. Often, as the sun tinted the western sky with pastel shades of pink, mauve, rose and lavender, there swept over my spirit an acute awareness of the gracious presence of God's own winsome Spirit. Communion between us was very personal, very private, very profound.

This was one of the reasons we had searched so long to find "Still Waters." I longed for those times when I could be still and know God. In the tender hours of twilight and daybreak, this did in fact take place.

At dusk, the wind would die. The lake surface became a smooth sheet of shining translucence, which caught and mirrored the breathtaking beauty of the burning skies. In summer, these desert skies flame and burn with blazing banners of tattered clouds. From horizon to horizon, their glory fills the vault of heaven. The still waters of the lake double and intensify this spectacle, until one's whole being pulses with profound awe and adoration. Only God could paint the clouds, the hills, the valley and the lake with such splendid strokes of pigment. No two evenings, no two dawns, were ever identical. The Master is an artist of enormous and infinite diversity.

At dawn, the eastern sky above the rock ramparts often glowed gold. This same metallic tint would wash over the cliffs and ridges all around us. Often they looked as if cast in bronze, fresh from the sculptor's hand. The beauty and glory of their grandeur was reflected in the lake.

Not a leaf would stir; not a ripple would rise on the water. The whole world lay still—serene, breathless, yet majestic.

There would then sweep over my soul that sublime and stirring assurance: "This is the day the Lord has made. I will rejoice and be glad in it" (*see* Psalms 118:24 LB).

It was a moment to relish!

Seven
Rain in the Desert

Yesterday was one of those dry, desperate days that can make the desert a dread. The leaves on the trees hung limp and wilted, unmoved by any stray eddy of air. The grass, bleached and gaunt and brittle from too much sun, broke in bits under my desert boots. It lay crushed and shattered wherever touched by the hard hooves of deer that had dashed across it. I had followed three bucks that took shelter from the searing sun. They sought the dense thickets of alder and black birch beside the lake. But even there, every move they made was amplified by the crack and crackle of brittle branches and dry twigs.

The heated air of the valley was close, oppressive and stifling. No birds rose up to sing against the sky, which was empty of their sounds. Nor did any take pleasure in winging against the wind, for there was none. The whole desert realm lay still, impassive, weighted down with the heaviness of heat.

The sun itself, so often friendly and warm and welcome, was now a terror and torment. The intensity of its light drove every living thing to seek shelter in the shade. Its fierce rays scorched the skin and shriveled the body. Even a plunge in the lake provided only momentary relief.

As the long, slow hours of the afternoon wore away, I flung myself down in the dappled shade of a sturdy sumac that grew at the water's edge. Yet even there, the heat was so stifling, so smothering, that my breath came in short pants. My head throbbed with pressure. Even the ground beneath my body was too hot, too hard, too gaunt to provide any comfort. So I rose and wandered about, almost in a stupor, longing for some sign, some signal that the weather might break.

There seemed to be none.

The sunset, brilliant and dramatic with its multihued desert clouds, seemed to hold promise of more sun the next day. Slowly its fingers of fire quenched the last smoldering shafts of light, and the day died in a gray ash of cloud clinging to the westerly sky.

Almost with a sigh of despair, I resigned myself to the thought of another day of desperate heat and desiccation. What else could one do but accept the weather as it came, whether blazing like a furnace or chilling as a blizzard?

But just before bedtime, my eyes caught a glimpse of misty gold rising through the silhouetted saskatoons on the high bank behind the cabin. The moon was mounting the sky, shrouded in a peculiar halo of fine-spun light. It could spell only one thing; there was moisture in the atmosphere. Perhaps rain was in the offing.

It was the sign I had been seeking.

It was the slender hope of a change.

And in that hope, I fell asleep, weary with heat.

Long, long before break of day, when I usually awake, there was a stirring in the leaves of the trees outside my window. A breeze began to rustle the limp foliage. Leaves rattled against one another, and on the rising wind, I heard the rolling, tumbling sounds of distant thunder.

The rain was coming!

Soon odd drops began to spatter on the roof above my head. The cabin has no ceilings; it is open beamed. Only satin-smooth cedar boards with shingles over their top stand between me and the sky. So the increasing tempo of the descending raindrops was music to my soul.

This is an ancient sound—the sound of rain falling on leaves, on bark, on grass, on rocks and soil. It is perhaps one of the most soothing and reassuring sounds upon the planet. It speaks of refreshment, relief and life from death.

There in the darkness of the night, in the wetness of the rain, in the cooling of the air, there was comfort. All the world—the little world of this desert valley—rested in quiet repose. The refreshment of the rain came, bringing total relaxation.

All was well.

And in that knowledge, I rolled over and fell asleep again. My sleep was deep and sweet and strong.

In my subconscious mind, there was the music of
moisture descending from above: a gift from God, my
Father.

Several hours later, I awoke again. A diffused light
filtered through the trees from an overcast sky. It was
still raining, but very gently, quietly. The raindrops
were barely audible on the deck outside. They scarcely
dimpled the surface of the lake. Yet everywhere there
was wetness, coolness and gladness.

Bird songs rang through the air with notes of crystal-
clear beauty. The meadowlarks on the dry sagebrush
benches flung their melodies into the morning light with
gay abandon. The songs splintered themselves on the
great bluffs and echoed off across the lake. Swallows
swept over the lake in graceful arcs, calling cheerfully to
their newly fledged broods to follow them in their swift
flight. The orioles chattered happily as they moved from
tree to tree in search of insects drowsy with dampness.

With the coming of the rain, shrubs and trees and grass
and reeds glowed emerald green. All their tissues were
taut and turgid with moisture. Even in the somber gray
light, they shone wet and smooth and satiny, charged
with fresh life from within. New vitality and dynamic
vigor moved in every living thing.

I slipped quietly out the door. Standing alone, inhaling deeply of the exquisite fragrance of soil wet with
rain, deep and profound gratitude welled up within me
for such a joyous interlude.

The rain had come!

All of us together were singing thanks to God.

Eight
Tame Trout

Our mountain lake, though only about three miles long and three-quarters of a mile wide, is a native habitat to some thirty-odd species of fish. This may or may not constitute somewhat of a record for so small a body of water. Not being an ardent fisherman, my knowledge of such things is rather meager.

In part, the prolific abundance of fish in the lake may be explained by the diversity of its character. A rather large river flows into one end. There, mud and silt carried down from the mountains by spring freshets has formed rich alluvial mud flats and warm-water shallows. In places, the lake is scarcely deep enough to float a canoe.

In these shallows there is a luxuriant growth of bulrushes, water lilies and assorted aquatic plants that provide certain species with ideal feed. Here, too, insect
populations proliferate, kept in control above the water
by the swooping birds and bats, while below the surface,
fish feed eagerly on the larvae and pupae of all sorts.

In other places, this same little lake is deep, dark and
very chill. Just below its outlet there are two gorgeous
and unique lagoons tucked away in a quiet curve of the
hills. These lagoons have the appearance of twin vol-
canic craters. There the water is very deep, very cold,
very blue and full of splendid deep-bodied bass.

We love to hike around these lagoons. They are much
more impressive than any man-made lakes. Encircling
their edges are steep banks of sandy desert soil. Acres of
wild flowers flourish here in spring and summer. Solid
banks of wild sunflowers blow in the hot breezes beneath the red-barked ponderosa pines. The effect is one
of a gigantic park, adorned by the brilliant hues of the
blue lagoons and the wash of gold on the desert benches,
all interspersed with the rugged, rusty trunks of the veteran pines.

In autumn, the same setting is changed to brilliant
reds and scarlets by the flaming banks of native sumac.
All of it is too beautiful, too striking to be adequately
portrayed by pen and paper. But it is here that the bass
and other lake fish feed along the shore and shelter in
the dark shadows of the trees that overhang the banks.

In front of our own cottage there are some beautiful
weed beds that grow in rich profusion. These bulrushes,
which blow and bend in the wind, provide ideal habitat
and cover for a wide array of birds and insects. Yet they

also are a favorite feeding ground for the fish. Giant carp, perch and sunfish frequent the area. Their great splashes breaking the surface have always fascinated me. It does me great good to know there is a flourishing fish population in the lake.

From time to time, trout feed fiercely near the surface. In their great rushes, they burst through the barrier of water, breaking out into clear air, their shining bodies arched in glorious silver arcs. Spray flies in the glinting sunlight as they splash down again. Ripples radiate far across the smooth water, leaving widening rings to remind us of their presence.

Just how prolific and numerous the trout were, we never fully realized until Cheri began to feed the fish. It all began with a dainty pair of spotted sunfish. They came into our tiny bay and began to stake out territory for their beds. Fiercely the little fish would attack and pursue any intruder. Steadily, day after day, they dug their beds, shed their eggs and sperm, then stood guard over their spawning ground.

Out of compassion and affection for the wee fish, Cheri began to scatter bread crumbs on the water. Her finny friends seemed glad of this unexpected bounty. But like so many things in life, one step soon led to another. One day, not only were the sunfish there, but also several small trout fingerlings. They, too, tasted the bread and loved it.

Not being an authority on fish behavior, I have no clear idea how the trout told their friends about the ready banquet of bread on our beach. But almost before we knew it, the first few fish soon increased to ten—then fifteen, twenty, up to thirty, then fifty or more—until I could no longer count their flashing, darting forms. At the last serious effort I made to take a census, there were well over seventy young trout swirling about beneath the surface.

Bread, it seemed to me, was not by any measurement the best food for fish. I gave the matter some serious thought and hit on the idea of providing our friends a high-protein food in the form of dog pellets. The results were utterly astounding. Their numbers increased even further, and the fish began to grow rapidly. In just a short time, they matured from slender fingerlings to fine, plump, pan-size trout.

It surprised us to see how quickly the trout learned to recognize our voices. They would come bursting to the surface whenever we walked out onto the rocks, calling to them or rattling the tin containing the pellets. To make sure all the fish would be fed, we scattered the food far and wide twice a day. This became a regular ritual, on which the trout thrived. It was also a novel experience for friends who came to visit us. Children, especially, were entranced and found endless delight in feeding our friends.

Deep down, I knew this happy arrangement would not last too long. The sharp eyes and keen senses of the loons, the grebes, the mergansers, soon alerted them to our concentration of trout. They came from all over the lake to raid this happy hunting ground. A smooth, slick dive, or a darting drive, a rapier thrust of their sharp beaks, and they would break water with a trout struggling between their mandibles.

But more than wild birds became aware of our trout. Fishermen in their canoes began to frequent our shore.

It was a clear signal for our hand-feeding to end. I refused to have our friends betrayed. They would do much better foraging afar on their own.

It was another example of how unwittingly, even in good faith, our best actions and intentions can misfire. It was a case of members of the wildlife fraternity becoming overly dependent on, and therefore vulnerable to, human behavior.

As the season wore on and late summer moved into fall, some of the trout would swim past the big timber where I stretched out in the sun. These were just passing visits. Their silver sides would catch the slanting rays of the sun glancing down through the clear, cool water. In their swift, smooth action I sensed a gracious salute of acknowledgement to us, who had sent them off to such a strong start in life.

Not all of them had survived the fierce attacks of the winged hunters. And some, too, had been snared by the deception of the fishermen's flies alighting on the lake. Yet those that now remained were firm and fat and fit for winter weather. We were all friends together, still, and for that I was glad.

There would be trout rushing to the surface until freeze-up. There would be the splash of their rising to ripple the lake. There would be the dark, concentric, ever-growing circles of moving water where they fed. And for all their sights and sounds that enlivened our world together, I was glad and grateful.

To me, the fish and turtles, the mink and muskrats, the beavers and birds, the coyotes and bears, the deer and mountain sheep were all fellows of blood and bone and sinew, who reveled and rejoiced in our mountain realm.

None of us dominated it or deprived the other of his share of it.

Each of us played our part in the finely strung web of life that enfolded us in a common joy of rich and hearty companionship. There was a sense of profound reverence and respect among us, each for the other. Our common ground and mutual interdependence guaranteed that none of us would abuse or exploit the other in greed or waste.

It has been ordained and ordered by our Father that we live in harmony with one another and with Him. It is possible to be at peace in life, and in very large and rich measure, we had found and fostered such serenity at "Still Waters."

Nine
August Wind

There are days in mid-August that come winging in on the wind with mysterious magic. Like nature's notes of prophecy, they foretell the coming fall. They are not true summer days, even though by the calendar, autumn may still be more than a month away.

Yesterday was one of those out-of-season times—a pure Indian summer interlude injected into the very heart of August heat. And I loved it. It stirred my inner spirit and set my emotions in rhythm with its own wild freedom.

During the night a heavy downpour—unexpected and sudden, driven by a strong weather system off the Pacific—pounded the shingles. The falling drops splat-

tered on leaves, bark, soil and stone in a steady murmur.
All the earth sounds were stilled, but for the symphonic
melody of a parched earth being soaked and scrubbed
and sloshed with streaming rivulets of rain.

In the dim half-light of the damp dawn, wraiths of
steamy vapor rose from the margin of the lake. They
wavered among the graceful green wands of the bulrushes, betraying where underground springs of warm
water bubbled below the surface of the lake.
Spellbound, I watched a trio of playful mergansers dash
and dart through this ghostlike scene, as if deliberately
dramatizing its eerie atmosphere.

There was something very primitive, very poignant,
yet delightfully arresting in the spectacle. Even the most
artistic director of a film could not have staged the setting any more dramatically. The soft, cotton-wool-like
mist moving formlessly among the swaying tule stems
was a remarkable backdrop against which the excitable
fish ducks put on their ecstatic performance.

Now one, then the other, then all three in unison
would streak across the water like torpedoes, leaving
wakes of white water behind them. In wild abandon,
they would dive below the surface, then come bursting
into view again.

Ecstatic with energy, they would stand erect, treading
water with their short feet, flapping their stubby wings
in self-applause. Somehow their whole show was an
open, hearty invitation to any onlooker to "Come on
in—the water is wonderful!"

This unplanned performance set the mood for the
whole day. It was a thrill to be alive—aware—open to
the powerful impulses of the earth.

As morning light touched the bold bluffs of Coyote

Rock, the gaunt slabs of stone shone smooth and wet. At first the rock faces looked as though they had been sheathed in the first fall of early snow. In the deceptive light playing through the clouds and overcast, the shining stone appeared white and soft. But it was not; a glance through the binoculars revealed only stark stone shining, sheathed in wetness.

The powerful south wind that had pushed the storm in overnight continued unabated. It began to break up the cloud cover. Soon warm summer sunlight streamed down through the torn and tattered canopy. It left a dappled patchwork of light and shadows flung across the landscape—a landscape that glowed and pulsed.

As the last fragments of cloud were pushed across the brown bluffs to the east, blue skies of breathless beauty and clarity arched overhead. No longer could I resist the strong pull to slip outside and soak up the sun in my favorite spot. There would not be many more days like this before frost and snow and ice locked this little valley in winter's cold grip.

At the very water's edge, just a few inches above the granite boulders, I had wedged a giant driftwood timber. Where it came from is unknown. Seldom, in these days of laminated beams, does one ever see a great fir log like this. Cut from a single monarch of a tree, it is twenty-six feet long, a foot thick and eighteen inches wide. It is an ideal sunbathing deck where, like a smooth, contented seal, I stretch out to take the sun and listen to the lap of water on stone a few feet from my face.

It was here I rested and relaxed, reveling in the symphony of earth's music that surrounded me. Instead of abating, the August wind gathered force and energy in its fists. Blowing hard from the southwest quarter, it stirred the lake and churned up charging whitecaps.

For such a small lake in such a sheltered valley, surrounded by high hills and bold bluffs, it was exciting to see the wild action of the water. Driven strongly, the waves would run hard, climb to a rising peak, then cascade down in white foam that hissed in the wind. The wash of the waves, the splash of water on the boulders about me and the wind in the trees around combined to make music that thrilled me to the depths. It was a melody of ancient origin, but it struck responsive notes deep in the spirit of a simple man, stretched out beneath its beat.

There was something wild, untamed, untaught in that wind music. It was not contrived or manipulated by man. This was the sort of melody that had been played out upon the planet long before the earliest men had thought of a woodwind instrument as simple as a reed flute cut from the stem of some marsh grass.

But there was more, much more than the majestic music of God's own making that morning. There was exquisite beauty of wondrous proportions cupped in my valley world.

The wind-wrought surface of the lake shone like beaten silver. A million points of blinding light bounced and danced in a brilliant ballet of abandon. They glided and pirouetted across the sparkling stage in exciting performance. Perhaps not another soul had stopped to pause and take in the show.

For me, it was a stirring day. It had etched itself indelibly on my memory. This was a precious interlude lifted from time, to be stored sacredly in the vault of remembrance. Humbly I bowed in awe and gave thanks.

Ten
Friends on the Wing

Living as close as we did to the lake and woods and wild hills around us, it was inevitable that some of our most intimate friends should be the birds. It is no small pleasure to have hundreds of birds of various species within a stone's throw of the windows. There was an intimacy—of sharing the same world of trees and water, cliffs and meadows—that is very rare.

For Cheri, in particular, the antics and behavior of the birds was a never-ending source of pleasure. She is an extremely acute and alert wildlife observer. The intense interest she displayed, often dashing from window to window to follow a bird's behavior, was often both joyful and hilarious to watch.

It was as if we had been admitted directly into the private lives of our feathered friends. Without fear or overshyness, they lived out their little lives in full view of our wondering eyes.

Those closest to us were a pair of beautiful barn swallows. With their shining plumage of gun-barrel blue and gun-stock brown, they circled the cottage in graceful swooping arcs. Quite obviously they were a young pair, mating for the first season. Their initial attempt to stick one of their mud-pellet nests to the cottage were clumsy and rather disastrous.

To help them out, I installed a small shelf just below the eaves and above one of the windows, where we could watch them. They accepted the site at once, and within a few days had a fresh nest, lined with feathers, ready for their brood to come.

They would be among the best of birds to control the mosquitoes. In fact, by midsummer there were literally scores of swallows swooping over the lake and around the water's edge. Any insect that dared to rise out of the tules or emerge from the shelter of the trees was promptly picked up in midflight.

The swallows' favorite perch was on our clothesline. Here they loved to sit and preen themselves, warbling contentedly. They are very vocal birds. Cheri would often stand at the open window, chattering to them in a happy exchange of mutual admiration. She kept me fully posted on the most recent and minute details of their activities.

In due course, the adults reared a strong and sturdy family of four fledglings. In just a few weeks, the young ones were swift of wing and sure of eye. They would come sweeping through the garden, to settle on the clothesline when their wings grew weary. As summer moved on, they were joined by scores of other young fliers emerging from nests all around the lake. Besides the barn swallows, some of which had nests on neighbors' houses, there were tree swallows and cliff swallows. All of them combined obviously consumed thousands upon thousands of insects in any single day. Because of this, our own lives beside the lake were infinitely more pleasurable than they would have been if persecuted by hordes of mosquitoes, flies and gnats.

I was tremendously impressed with the calm courage of the swallows. Fearlessly they would attack larger predator birds that intruded on their territory. The magpies, crows and blue jays that dared to invade the environs of "Still Waters" were pursued in fierce flight, with the swallows sweeping down upon them like diving Stukas in deadly combat.

Another species of bird that brought flashing gaiety to our garden was the western Bullock's orioles. They are not only very colorful birds, adorned in beautiful black and gold plumage, but also very noisy. Their harsh cries and incessant calls, especially of the young, enlivened the woods and sang through the trees all the time they were with us.

Several pair nested within fifty yards of the cottage. Their intricate nests, woven from threads, string and slender stalks of grass, were suspended from the topmost branches of the native poplars. There they swung and swayed in the wind, appearing at a distance to be rather precarious, but close at hand revealing wondrous design of great strength.

I am fully aware that it is customary for the so-called scientific community to dismiss the extraordinary behavior of birds with the shrug of a shoulder and the all-encompassing word *instinct*. But for those of us who have lived in close intimacy with the wilds, this is just not good enough. Whence these so-called instincts? Whence these incredibly intricate and efficient behavior patterns, which so perfectly adapt a species to its particular environment? Whence the consummate skill, expertise and intelligence that enables individuals within the bird community to capitalize on and use the materials at hand to survive in its special setting?

Let me illustrate. One day Cheri hung a tattered piece of cloth to dry on the clothesline. Actually it was a duster with frayed edges. It had been there only a few hours when the orioles decided it would provide perfect nesting material. With great ingenuity and no little dexterity, they would fly down and cling to the cloth, tearing long threads out of the material with beak and claw.

This was an intricate process, and so I suggested that we cut strips of a softer material and hang them on the line for their benefit. Strange to say, it was a futile gesture. The orioles rejected the strips immediately. If they were to use man-made fabric to fashion their nests, it would have to be of their own choosing, unraveled by their own beaks and claws.

Again one must ask: Whence the intelligence to even know that cloth contained long, thin threads suited to their needs? Whence the capacity to ascertain that this material, even if obtained by great labor, surpassed grass in strength and durability? Whence the will and resolve to incorporate cloth, thread or string into a structure that ordinarily was fashioned only from plant fibers?

Obviously there is much more at work here than mere blind instinct. There is an element of thought, of deduction, of discovery, of determination that goes far beyond mere animal behavior. In all of it, we sensed a dimension of delightful supernatural design. It was not something merely acquired during the evolutionary process. It was evidence of our Father's care for His earth children.

By midsummer, the trees were literally alive with vigorous young orioles flitting and flashing through the foliage. They were pursuing all sorts of caterpillars, earwigs, ants and wood insects that flourished amid the labyrinth of twigs and leaves. It was a reassuring thought that the community of common birds all around us was so happily controlling the native insect population, which would otherwise have decimated the trees and shrubs that made our surroundings so beautiful.

As the seasons came and went, so did the birds. There was a steady succession of various species moving around us in gentle harmony with the length of day and time of year. Chickadees and nuthatches, warblers and juncos, robins and towhees—to name but half-a-dozen kinds—sang and whistled their way through the trees and brush in their tireless search for food for their families.

In all of this, we sensed the wondrous web of life, whose delicate strands embraced all of us. Indirectly and directly, we were all interdependent. The welfare and contentment of birds, forest, shrubs, and man himself were intertwined. Each of us was contributing something of value to the common good, while at the same time each derived that which was essential for his enjoyment and enduring existence.

This was one of those basic *beginnings* we had sought from the start in our search for "Still Waters." There was a fundamental feeling of harmony, repose and goodwill in all the natural life around us. None of us, whether birds, vegetation or man, were imposing ourselves upon another. Rather, the atmosphere around our home was one of quiet contentment. In this environment there was a natural balance, unmolested by crude or thoughtless behavior.

This may sound rather far-out and farfetched for those whose lives are lived in the labyrinth of a modern metropolis. But for us at "Still Waters," this was that unique and special ingredient that made our life there a quiet, gentle, unforgettable adventure.

Eleven
The Little Stray

It was a warm September morning, aglow with mellow sunlight and splashed by autumn colors. The birches were beginning to blaze, with bronze leaves fluttering in the wind. The sumacs on the hills flamed scarlet among the gray sage. A golden-breasted meadowlark filled the countryside with rippling notes of contentment that seemed to rise in joy to the blue, blue skies.

But all was not at peace. A sad and discordant sound suddenly came across the grassy glade of the vacant land north of us. From out of the wild tangle of trees and brush along the lake came a plaintive, sad, melancholy cry that sounded half-feline, half-human. It was a persistent, forlorn, pathetic sound, like someone lost and pleading for help.

My wife and I hurried to the edge of the underbrush. There a labyrinth of intertwined wild rosebushes, Oregon grape, snow berries and poison oak grew in wild profusion beneath the birches.

We could see a small, slim, shy animal coming through the undergrowth. The first glimpse or two made us think it might be a weasel. But when she broke out into the open sunlight, we saw it was a skinny, half-starved kitten. She was snow-white, like a weasel in winter dress. Only a smudge of dark fur between her ears tinged the whiteness of her coat. She carried an enormous, fluffy, white tail, out of all proportion to her slim and shrunken body—now only skin and bones.

We called to her. Her response was to come bounding out of the bush. Her eyes—peculiar eyes, one brilliant blue, the other an orb of gold—flashed with fear and apprehension. At first she fled at our sight, but with patience and perseverance, Cheri was finally able to pick her up. Half-starved, having survived only on insects, the odd dead bird and wild berries, she was a pathetic little bundle of white fluff. Like thousands of other domestic pets, she had been dropped in the country, to fend for herself.

This callous abandonment of city-bred animals in the country is one of the cruel and heinous crimes of our much-vaunted modern society. Men and women, who lack courage and compassion, coldheartedly dump their feline and canine friends at the side of the road, then blithely drive away, leaving them to struggle for survival. This has become such a common practice by our populace that thousands of stray dogs and cats have to be destroyed every year by rangers, wardens and those who find them in their forlorn plight.

We picked up the kitten and carried her home to the cottage. It was almost like gathering up a bundle of cotton batten. The mere skeleton, with thin flesh stretched over her bony frame, was concealed only by the fluff of her white fur. At first it seemed she might not even survive. She was so emaciated that anything she tried to eat or drink only resulted in violent diarrhea. But Cheri had owned and cared for cats before, and her tender care began to pay off.

It quickly became apparent that this was no ordinary alley cat. She carried the royal blood of both Siamese and Persian aristocracy in her veins. In fact, she seemed to combine the best of both breeds in her unique makeup.

Having owned and trained only dogs all my life, it was a brand-new and rather unusual adventure to have a cat in the house. I had always been told that cats were arrogant, independent, proud and aloof. For that reason there had never been any great desire to have one share my life. But now there was really very little choice. This little white waif, of ghostlike appearance, had come into our care, and I was determined to see she would get a chance to enjoy her life with us at "Still Waters."

I soon christened her Oddy, because both her appearance and behavior were so odd. In time she began to recognize this name and would come when called by it.

Very quickly we discovered that she was an unusually alert and intelligent animal. She could be taught and trained as readily as any dog. What was even more impressive was her great and unbounded affection. She quickly dispelled all of my misgivings about the arrogant aloofness of cats. She showed beyond doubt that she was capable of reciprocating any love showered upon her.

She enjoyed our companionship and quickly made herself at home in our company. She loved to crawl up on our laps, purring so loudly the muted rumblings could be heard clear across the room. Sometimes she would stand on my lap, place her immaculate white front feet on my chest and reach up to touch noses. I guess this is the way a cat kisses. At any rate, she reveled in it so much she would tread my chest ecstatically, like someone kneading dough with deep delight.

Her behavior reminded me again and again of that of a dog. She would follow me around the garden. She loved to climb up on my back when I laid down in the sun for an afternoon siesta. She would be waiting on the lawn when we came home in the car, eager to greet us with a contented mew and bounds of delight at our approach. She snuggled down between us on the chesterfield when the day's work was done and we listened quietly to classical music in the evening.

Fine music seemed to have a special appeal to her. Often she would cock her head to one side and listen intently, like the dog with his ear to the gramophone on the old records. High notes on the flute or violin, or from a beautiful soprano voice, especially stirred her with pleasure. She would open her eyes wide, cock her ears and pay special attention, as though this was her favorite taste in symphonic fare.

Oddy, after her first few faltering days, soon began to blossom under our loving care. She started to put on weight rapidly. Her frame filled out, her fur began to glow and shine with well-being. And she took great pains to keep her coat immaculate.

She was a wild, free spirit, out-of-doors. She literally danced and tumbled about the grounds, like a windblown leaf. In two titanic leaps, she could bound up a tree with lightning alacrity. It was never a surprise to see her working her way across the slender branches above us with utter impunity. She never showed any fear of falling. And, unlike many cats, whatever she climbed she found equally easy to descend with great leaps and bounds, as if built of spring steel.

Her enormous agility and swiftness made her a formidable hunter. Besides all the food we lavished upon her, she augmented her diet with a steady toll of mice, shrews, moles and small birds she collected in the bush around us. It was a perfect place to hunt. She would steal through the undergrowth, her tail tip twitching with excitement, to pounce with intense speed upon her prey. Soon not a mouse was to be seen. She had made a clean sweep of the entire environs of the cottage. With winter approaching, this was a real benefit, for with freezing nights in the fall, the mice would soon move into the cottage, attracted by its warmth, shelter and fragrance of fresh food.

Contrary to much of what I had been told about cats, Oddy loved the water. She would spend hours working her way along the lake edge. The reflection of her own face in the mirrorlike surface fascinated her. She loved to dip her paws in the refreshing coolness, then shake them off vigorously. Often she sat entranced, watching the sunfish and small trout that swam past her only a few inches from her long, eagerly twitching white whiskers. How she would have loved to snatch one of these tasty morsels from the lake.

The wild ducks and geese also fascinated her. At dusk they would sometimes swim in close to shore, where she crouched, watching them intently. It was a mutual game that both ducks and cat seemed to enjoy. The ducks would swim as close as possible to her, as if enticing her to come out and play. They knew precisely how close they could come to her without being pounced upon. In convoylike formation, they would swim close, streaming past her, quacking in a provocative way that would start her blood boiling and her tail twitching.

When at last they had taunted her to extremity, they would turn tail, flip water in her face and leave her to fume in furious frustration.

But on balance, she did not lose all her games with birds. Morning after morning I would find scattered heaps of feathers strewn on the lawns where she had gorged herself on the warm flesh of a freshly caught bird. It soon became clear that she was a relentless hunter. If we wanted to enjoy the birds around "Still Waters," she would have to find another home.

This was a tough decision for us. Like so many things in life, there was no simple, single solution. Try as we might to discourage her from her death-dealing ways, she persisted in pursuing her prey. In so far as she could see, anything that moved was legitimate prey. It mattered not whether it wore fur or feathers—she would stalk it fiercely.

As it so happened, this really led to her ultimate undoing, for inevitably her own feminine presence soon led to visits from other cats much larger than herself. The nights of quietness would be shattered and splintered like broken glass with the awful screams of cats in combat. Oddy would arch her back, raise her hackles and defy any interloper to take another step onto her territory. She fought fiercely and courageously.

The final consequence was that some mornings she came to the door with blood upon her face, scratches upon her lips and a rumpled coat that betrayed fierce fights with others of her feline fraternity. We knew that sooner or later she would end up being pregnant or badly mauled by some belligerent visitor.

As it so happened, both came true. Oddy began to gain weight very quickly, so we suspected kittens were on the way. Her kittenish antics gave place to a much more placid and sedentary life-style. She would spend long hours stretched out in the most humanlike poses on the big armchair near my desk. It was hilarious to see her lying on her back, arms crossed, as if she were a little old man in his eighties, snoring up a storm.

Then one night she was severely mauled. A few days later, an enormous swelling developed on her back. It was so painful she would not let us touch her. Morose and ill, she simply dozed intermittently. She refused to eat or drink. Her eyes grew dull, and her energy drained away. There was only one thing to do; we had her put to rest for the sake of mercy.

Like a bright comet, this little white visitor had swept through our lives with gaiety and affection. She left behind a starry trail of happy memories. I was glad we had shared so freely of our affection. " 'Tis better to have loved and lost, than never to have loved at all."

In the brief years of our human experience, some of us sense and *know* that our lives have been touched by the divine in diverse ways. Our heavenly Father does not limit Himself to human agencies to speak to His own.

In Psalms 19:1, the ancient bard wrote, without a moment's hesitation, "The heavens declare the glory of God; and the firmament sheweth his handywork."

And it is just as valid to say that there are occasions when He uses animals to minister to our deepest needs, just as He does with other human beings. Observe the comfort, cheer and companionship that comes to children and the very aged from their pets. The love and loyalty of dogs, cats, horses and other domestic creatures sometimes puts human unpredictability to shame.

A very aged gentleman lives a few hundred yards down the lake from us. His twilight years are enriched and embroidered by the gentle stroll he takes every day with his faithful old Blackie. Together the two of them shuffle softly down our gravel road, soaking up sunshine, inhaling fresh air and exercising their aging joints. For both man and dog, it is the special interlude of the day.

In a similar manner, it is my conviction that Oddy was sent to us at a very special time in our lives, to share briefly a sorrowful interlude that weighed heavily on our spirits. It was in the sadness of difficult days that this gay-spirited cat came to us, like a gift of gaiety from God. Her warmth, her affection, her devotion, her fun, her hilarious humor, helped to ease us through a very trying time.

Often, as I romped with her in front of the fire or caressed her silky white coat as she lay on my lap, I knew this was no ordinary interlude. In His awareness and sensitivity to our special need, Oddy had been sent to minister to a man and woman in sorrow.

I would look down at her graceful, gentle white form and know she was like an "angel unawares" in our company.

Twelve
Wild Waterfowl

The lake that laps on the little sand beach at our doorstep is home to a myriad of waterfowl. It has, across the years, been established as a wildlife sanctuary. Here shotguns do not roar out death to the ducks and geese that flash across our skies. Nor do outboard motors disturb the gentle tranquility of the waters.

There is a wooded island at the lower end of the lake that has become the favorite nesting ground for the Canada geese. Safe from four-legged predators, the goslings can be assured of a safe launch into life. Last year some 400 geese were hatched on the lake. Day and night the wild cries of their coming and going filled the skies, to echo across the valley from ridge to ridge.

The Canada goose is an unusually wary and intelligent bird. The social behavior within any given flock is complex, tightly knit and fiercely maintained. The birds are exceedingly loyal to each other and to their young. The interrelationship of the birds is maintained by almost-continuous conversation, which I call "goose gossip."

It came as a distinct surprise to me to discover that the geese gabble and call to one another through the night. On bright moonlit nights, when the lake is a shimmering sheet of silver, their cries are a cacaphony that resounds through the valley with remarkable resonance. Again and again, their goose talk has awakened me from my sleep and drawn me to the window to watch their dark forms silhouetted against the silver sheen of the water.

Because of this, I suspect that geese sleep much more during the day than they do at night. With sentinels on guard, they slip their heads beneath their wings and rest undisturbed.

The size of the young broods of goslings is really astonishing; even more so when pairs combine in intimate clans for mutual protection and sharing of parental duties. It is for this reason that sometimes there may be as many as sixty or seventy bouncing balls of yellow fluff following in the wake of only two or three adults. They are guarded zealously and fearlessly. An angered pair of geese makes a formidable foe. Their flashing eyes, darting beaks and hammering wings will drive off most predators in short order.

The rapid rate at which the young geese mature is almost beyond belief. In the first few weeks, if feed and forage is plentiful, the goslings will actually more than double their weight every day. They relish short, green, tender grass and dandelions. In fact, adult geese are so addicted to dandelions that they will go great distances and risk real danger to dine on this unusual delicacy.

Two or three times, flocks of the geese decided to pay our little lawn a passing visit. Its emerald green grass was a tremendous temptation. In a matter of minutes, their sickle-sharp beaks had cut the grass to the ground, almost to the very roots. As if this was not enough, it seemed every one of the more than 200 geese that strutted about the place felt constrained to defecate on the lawn. The result can be well imagined.

When this had occurred several times, I decided enough was enough. In desperation, I stretched a long length of rope across the entrance to our little beach, about a foot above the water. From it we suspended slender strips of gaudy cloth. It looked exactly like a miniature farmer's fence erected in the lake. It worked like magic! For the remainder of the season, not a goose dared to trespass past it. So peace came again, while the geese gabbled happily just offshore in the weed beds where they loved to feed.

Learning to fly was a major milestone in the lives of the maturing juveniles. As they approached adulthood, they would expend enormous energy flapping their wings, treading water, trying to take off.

Sometimes they would stand on shore, stretch themselves full length, beat the air boisterously, then race along the beach, endeavoring to rise on the wind. It was all very stimulating, exciting and hilarious to watch. These experimental first flights were accompanied with exultant honking and ecstatic cries of delight. To finally break free and become fully airborne was a feat that called for tumultuous celebration.

Stretching, flapping, treading water, spray flying, rising above the lake in faltering first flights, they made the whole valley ring with their cries of conquest. They were on wing! They were away!

In very remarkable truth, this was so in more ways than one. For in just a few fleeting days, the entire lake suddenly seemed to be alive with long, wavering lines of geese flying just a few feet above its surface. Back and forth, up and down its length, they would beat their way. Night and day the sound of their practice flights upwind was carried to us on the shifting breezes.

Then suddenly a strange stillness descended on the scene. Almost overnight, most of the geese were gone. In response to an ancient urge, most of them left for faraway places on the prairies, where feed was more plentiful. The wise old adults had been there before. They knew all about the great grain fields, the open marshes, the potholes and the banqueting grounds of the stubble land.

Whence this wisdom? Whence the courage and stamina to vault the giant mountain ranges that reared their snowy ridges and rocky ramparts into the flyways of the birds? Whence the strength in birds so young, to beat their wings against the winds with weary muscles and straining tendons, hour after hour, across uncharted forests, valleys, rivers and ranges?

There was a majestic mystery in these transmountain migrations. In that mystery I stood awed in quiet wonderment. This is my Father's world. He made it; He sustained it; He kept it; He cared; He knew if one fledgling fell along the way.

Besides the geese, there were numerous other waterfowl. Loons and grebes and ducks all nested along the shores, secreting their nests amid the tules or in the dense brush growing along the banks.

Of these, one pair of mallards especially interested us. The female was an unusual albino bird. She was courted ardently by several drakes. Finally one night, under the full moon, she was mated by a monstrous drake. Cheri watched the whole pageantry with intense excitement, reporting all the romantic details to me the next day.

In due course, the hen emerged from the bulrushes with nine ducklings in tow. She proved to be a most indulgent and alert parent. Her young ones flourished under her careful protection and by summer's end were even larger than she was. The family made a handsome flotilla as they dabbled about in front of the cottage.

It astonished us how nonchalantly these ducks faced rough weather on the lake. Even when stiff winds stirred the waves up into racing whitecaps, the little ones bounced about on the surface with ease and no apparent fear.

The ducks enjoyed coming into our tiny beach. There they would strut on the sand, gather gravel for their crops, then pause to preen their feathers in the warm morning sun. If perchance Oddy was around, they would drift just out of reach, then tantalize her to come after them with jeering quacks, as if to say, "Can't catch us—can't catch us!"

When autumn closed quietly over the countryside, the lake ducks were joined by other flights from farther north. The swift swish of their wings whistled through the still air. In the brilliant, brittle light of Indian summer, the flash of their forms shone silver and white against the blue of the lake, the blue of the misty hills, and the blue of the autumn sky.

Few artists have ever been able to fully capture the elemental rapture of this pristine pageantry on canvas. In part, this is because of the electric action, the scintillating sequence of massed bodies, in perfect formation, sweeping across the sky in wild glory.

Anyone who has stood alone at sunset or dawn, watching the evening and dawn flights of waterfowl, will know there is an aura of beauty and wonder here that no book can adequately capture. They are rich moments of ecstasy. They are magnificent intervals of time, which the passing years cannot erase from the memory.

This is but one of our Father's gracious gifts to us, His earth children. We are richer for the company of our feathered friends. We know it and, in humble, hearty contentment, give happy thanks.

One of my favorite birds on the lake is our neighbor the loon. Often quite a shy bird, those which nest in our area have become rather tame and less retiring in their habits. The loon is a large bird, beautifully adorned in brilliant black and white plumage of dramatic design. They are accomplished fishermen, of remarkable prowess in pursuing the trout and perch that share their watery world. They can dive to great depths and remain underwater for long periods of time.

There is a silken-smooth quality to a loon's movement in the water. There is a blending of body, plumage and fluidly flowing grace. When a loon dives, the water is scarcely stirred. The bird simply slides and glides out of sight in one smooth, subtle submersion. The same is true when he surfaces, scarcely rippling the water as his graceful form slips up out of the lake in a lovely arc.

Best of all, at least to me, is the long, lilting call of the loon. This cry carries across the lake in lonely, forlorn notes that spell *wilderness*. There is a wildness quality, a melancholy mood, a nostalgic note in this bird's unbridled call. It sends chills and thrills up my nerves. It spells out untamed places and untamed hours.

Being a son of the wilds, I find in it a bond and harmony with all things wild and wonderful.

Thirteen
Thanksgiving

In Canada, Thanksgiving comes as a very festive occasion in the most mellow month of the year. October—with its blue hazy days, its glowing golden dress and its stillness after the stressful summer—provides a perfect setting for this winsome celebration.

This year, Thanksgiving was extra special.

We were sharing it with dear, dear friends, whose feet had traveled far—very far—down the twilight trail of life. Despite the many years that had come and gone across the horizons of their lives, they still stood straight, sturdy and shining in spirit. They were people of the land, who had laid out their lives in selfless love for the downtrodden, impoverished natives of Haiti.

But now they were back home. Like the hunter home from the hills, they relaxed quietly and contentedly in the knowledge and comfort of work well done.

Early in the day, Cheri began to busy herself about the kitchen. There was a turkey to stuff and truss. There were vegetables to prepare with care. Yellow yams (sweet potatoes), a staple food of the Haitian peasants and a favorite dish of our friends, would be baked and smothered in sweet, sugary sauce. A crisp, fresh salad, made from the overflowing abundance of garden vegetables given to us by generous friends and neighbors, would garnish the table.

To top off the meal, there was pumpkin pie to prepare. This would be relished with delicious tea, brewed from the clear, cold spring water that flowed into our cottage.

As Cheri sang about the house, filling its rooms with her happy tunes, I went to search for special firewood to fuel the fireplace. Perhaps, if I was fortunate, I would find some flaming fall foliage to decorate the big-beamed living room.

I did not have to go far. On a dry, sagebrush bench back of the cottage, I followed a trail that led up to the toe of a giant rock slide. Across the centuries, frost and sun, wind and weather had worked on the towering cliffs above, breaking off gigantic slabs of stone and shale. The tons of brown and gray rock thundering down the cliffs had sheared off several firs and pines, which had rooted themselves at random in this rugged terrain.

For uncounted seasons, the broken trees had lain shattered on the slopes. Exposed to the scorching desert sun and scarce winter snows, the wood had turned silver-gray with age. The soft layers decomposed slowly, leaving behind only the pitch-impregnated limbs and knots and roots. These made superb firewood.

Searching for old, bone-hard branches and pitchy pine knots is like searching for precious minerals. The prospector is stimulated and driven on by the dream of discovery. For in those fragments of fuel, as in some precious ore, there is locked up the enormous, painstaking processes of nature that took place long, long years ago.

I moved, almost in a spirit of reverence, across the broken boulders and tortured talus. Here and there, wedged in among the tumbled rocks, were gaunt, gray branches and scattered fragments of roots and knots, which would flame to life in our fireplace.

The accumulated energy of a hundred summer suns locked within the pitchy wood would be released in bursts of red, orange and blue flames. The pent-up power of solar heat would crack and burst its bonds as the silver-gray wood turned to glowing red coals, hot as the choicest of coal.

Carefully, I climbed about the base of the granite cliffs. Bit by bit I gathered up armfuls of the prized fuel. It was brittle and broke readily when hammered against a jagged stone. There was no need for either axe or saw. This was a simple hunting ritual, primitive as earliest man, done readily without recourse to tools of any sort.

As I gathered up the beautiful, broken, weathered wood, a sense of having stepped back in time swept over me. The ancient instinct of the race came over me. I was back to basics. The strength of my own muscles, the keenness of my own eyes, the bounty of the earth about me, were the guarantee of a good fire and good cheer.

The wood collected, I began to look about for some

colorful foliage to decorate our rustic living room. My eye fell upon a distant flash of scarlet sumac. Most of the leaves had already fallen quietly among the dry bunch grass beneath the bushes. But here and there a few stray plants, growing in more-sheltered spots among the giant house-sized boulders, held their scarlet leaves in brave defiance of the elements. Sun and frost and vagrant breezes had not yet stripped their staghorn branches bare.

With great care, as painstakingly and precisely as if I were selecting exotic plants in an expensive florist shop, I chose several clusters of gay leaves. Their colors ranged from deep-rich scarlet hues to somber purple, from burnt orange to pale pink. They would make a handsome floral arrangement in any home.

As a final flourish, I plucked a few stalks of pungent rabbit brush, a desert plant whose brilliant golden sprays bloom at their best in late fall. Like the wild asters and goldenrod, these were the last salute of the long flowering season, which in this dry terrain stretches from late February to mid-October.

Happy in heart, singing in spirit, I bore my bounty home. As I opened the cottage door, the aroma of baking sweet potatoes and tender turkey tantalized my taste buds. It would be a delicious dinner, prepared with love and goodwill.

Sitting around the round wooden table that evening, all of us were engulfed in an atmosphere of warmth, love and gratitude to God, our Father. Out of His generosity and bounty, our lives had overflowed with good things and rich friendships. The sweet satisfaction of knowing that His great hand had been upon us, bestowing blessings beyond our desiring, humbled our hearts and drew us to Him in gratitude.

Cheri had placed a pretty candle in the center of the table. Its base was decorated with green sprigs of fragrant juniper. The gentle glow of the candlelight played upon the faces of our friends. They were people at peace. There was contentment there that came welling up from the inner depths of spirits in harmony with God, in harmony with each other and in harmony with us. It sparkled in their eyes and shone in their smiles.

When the feast was finished, we gathered around the fireplace. The silver-gray wood, which only an hour or two before lay bare and bleached upon the mountain, burst into blazing life. Its flames danced and played about the knots and burls, before leaping gaily up the chimney. Its warmth radiated into the room, warming the walls of cedar, enfolding us in "living" heat, unlike that produced by gas, electricity or oil.

Our friends reveled in its gaiety. They relaxed in its friendly atmosphere. At ease and joyous, we shared old stories and joined in hearty laughs, allowing the mellow memories of former times to engulf us in goodwill.

The old gentleman recalled how, as a young lad growing up on a Pennsylvania farm, he had gone to the hills in search of pine knots for their family fires. He, too, knew all about the magic and mystique of finding these pitch-laden prizes buried deep in the old pine woods.

As he recalled his boyhood escapades, a misty, wondrous light flooded his face. He was living youth again—the life of his boyhood days, with suntanned cheeks and bare feet. Never before had I seen him so handsome, so utterly alive, so wondrously well. It was as if forty summers had slipped from his shoulders. He stood strong again, erect and sturdy as a sapling of young manhood.

Cheri, in her generous, loving, gay way, offered to play a few pieces she was just learning on the organ. It was golden music, especially melodious because it was homemade with deep affection. The songs started the elderly lady's toes to tapping. Almost before we knew it, she offered to try a tune or two. In all her long years, her fingers had never touched an organ. But that Thanksgiving eve, there flowed from her heart and hands wondrous music of her own making. It was akin to a rebirth, a renewal, a recapturing of her gentle girlhood.

As time came for them to take their leave, I walked with them up the drive beneath the arching trees. There was a spring to their steps and a joy to their souls that refreshed my own spirit. We had shared and drunk deeply together from the deep delight of this day.

All of our hearts were aglow with true thanksgiving to God, our Father.

Fourteen
Beautiful Black Birches

Never lose an opportunity for seeing anything
    that is beautiful;
For beauty is God's handwriting—a wayside
    sacrament.
Welcome it in every fair face, in every fair sky,
    in every fair flower,
And thank God for it as a cup of His blessing.
                                RALPH WALDO EMERSON

Last evening, after a long, misty day of mountain rain, I looked out upon the lawn, and saw it lay carpeted in gold. Thousands upon uncounted thousands of tiny, shiny birch leaves, gilded with wetness, glistened on the green grass. Lying there in their myriads, they formed a wondrous irregular floral pattern, fashioned from tiny bits of life similar in design.

No two leaves, out of the millions that fell from the birch branches, were identical. Each was a unique structure of intricate complexity that now neared the end of its short-lived life span. For though the leaves no longer clung to the birch limbs, supporting the tree with their sustenance, the fabric of their flaming tissues would now begin to decompose upon the ground. Their cellular structure would contribute to the buildup of the rich black humus of the earth in which the black water birches thrived beside the lake.

For uncounted eons of time, the birches and poplars, the alders and willows, the red osier dogwoods and rose thickets, which flourished in the damp soil along the lakeshore, had made their annual contribution to its smooth, dark soil. Across the centuries, since the last giant glacier that carved this valley from granite rock had gone, the little trees had taken over soil building in this lovely spot.

As I cleared the virgin sod and spaded the loamy land for my garden this autumn, I could see in my mind's eye the long history of this gentle ground. Behind the gaunt blue ridges of receding ice lay a barren wasteland of glacial duff and rounded rocks. The finer till had been milled finer than any man-made mill could ever grind it, beneath the titanic raspings of ice shod with coarse teeth of fragmented rock imbedded in its blueness.

Century after century, in the brief, all-too-short summers of these northerly latitudes, stray seeds of dwarf arctic birch and northern willow had fallen upon the barren landscape. Here and there a hardy seedling of these pioneer trees—along with wild dwarf blueberries, mountain avens and some tough fireweed—took root in the rocky landscape.

Imperceptibly at first, but with increasing vigor, this persistent plant community began to clothe the bleak landscape with greenery in summer and brilliant color in autumn. The residue of their brief summer growth was quickly buried beneath long winters of snow, where it decayed. Slowly but steadily there was a buildup of thin soil, soon to be invaded by larger trees and more-luxuriant shrubs.

The eight or ten inches of velvet-smooth black soil that my shovel sliced through had taken ten thousand years to accumulate. Century upon century, there had gently accumulated layer upon layer of fallen leaves, dead twigs, decaying roots and shredded bark. Bacteria, soil organisms, insects, earthworms and fungi had found a fertile field in which to flourish. Each in its own quiet way contributed to the decomposition of the plant material. Each added the offscourings and residue of its own unique life force to the fabric of the earth.

In subsequent years, the dwarf vegetation was replaced and supplanted by larger and more-vigorous trees and shrubs. With the gradual advent of warmer seasons, earlier springs and fewer frosty days, the beautiful black birch, western poplars, mountain alders and red osier dogwood struck root in this sun-kissed valley.

To me, the graceful, slim-limbed western water birch, more commonly called the *black birch*, is one of our most beautiful mountain trees. It reminds me of the British name of endearment for their birches—"Lady of the Woods."

This tree is not attractive because of its scale or size. It has a most unusual growth form. Anywhere from six to twenty, or even more, slender trunks spring from a single root system. These dark, chocolate-colored stems radiate outwards at slanting angles from the center, each stretching toward the sun in a different direction. Where the tree is not cramped or constricted by competition from its fellow forest trees, it forms a striking vase shape.

The luxuriant black birch that dominates the front lawn of "Still Waters" is a classic example of this sturdy tree at its beautiful best. Its glistening brown trunks tower upward and outward to some forty or fifty feet. Its intertwining slender limbs and branches form a majestic canopy, outspread to the sky like an enormous umbrella of greenery.

So dense is its growth of fine twigs and dainty, heart-shaped leaves, that chickadees, nuthatches and warblers can work their way through it without being seen. As they search its labyrinth of foliage for insects, only their chirping calls and the steady dropping of tree debris disclose their whereabouts. In summer these trees form a splendid shield against the hot desert sun. In their shadow, the grass lies green and moist and cool: a pleasant spot to sit quietly and listen to the wind play through the slender, drooping limbs that hang down in handsome, graceful pendants.

The black birch never grows big enough to provide logs for lumber. At best, a veteran will measure about one foot across at its base. But for fireplace fuel, this hardy tree has no rival. It burns hot and clean. Its glowing coals give off heat equal to the best of coal. And when the winter woodpile contains a goodly share of this wood, the happy woodsman knows he can count on a score of contented evenings before his open hearth.

With careful, loving husbandry, the black birch is a tree that will perpetuate itself almost indefinitely. If care is taken to remove only the largest and most mature trees from a clump, other young ones immediately spring up from the root system to replace them. The foliage of these tender new shoots is a delicate olive green, quite distinct from the darker shade of the mature leaves.

The skilled woodsman with a kindly eye and understanding spirit will saw off the tree he cuts in such a way as not to mar the beauty of the younger stems that remain. I try to cut the trunk at an acute angle that blends in with the outward-growing tree form. And if the white wound is carefully painted over with dark-chocolate coating, it not only forestalls decay and insect invasion, but enables the tree to quickly heal over without distorting its elegant beauty.

Few are the trees found anywhere which lend so much beauty to lakeshore or stream side. They love water and are always found close to it—hence the name *water birch*. Their foliage, like fine filagree, is never found far from the sound of water, whether wavelets lapping on a sandy beach or the laughter of a stream tumbling over its stony course. Their long limbs sway in the wind, as if beating time to the water music about them.

In winter their intricate pattern of interlaced branches and twigs, shining black, stand out distinctly against the snow. In spring their hue changes to a ruddy, red glow as the rising sap swells the buds and streams through the slender twigs at the tips. In summer they are a gorgeous

mass of greenery, pulsing and vibrant in the brittle sunlight. Their roots are deep in dampness, their heads are
held proudly aloft. In autumn they glow like gold
against the blue haze and clear skies of Indian-summer
days.

It is then I go softly in search of the glistening mush-
rooms that grow about their base. And it is then I gather
up huge armfuls of their bronze leaves to build my com-
post pile. To me, black birches are beautiful.

Fifteen
Mountain Glory

Our little lake lies nestled among giant, rugged hills. In most countries they would be called mountains. They thrust their ragged ramparts, ridge upon rocky ridge, up to five-, six- and seven-thousand-foot heights.

Unlike some mountains, these rise one above the other in gigantic steps, one broken bench above the next. Colossal rock cliffs; breath-stopping canyons, cut through solid stone; bold bluffs of broken boulders; open, sweeping sagebrush flats; grassy slopes and thick-timbered ridges; all are interspersed in a wondrous variety of terrain.

Few places anywhere in the world offer such diversity

of scenery and landscape in so small a compass. Within a radius of twenty miles of my cottage door, one can pass through the lush greenery of the lakeshore, with its marshes and alder thickets; into desert country, with cactus and greasewood; up to open parkland, where ponderosa pines and juniper predominate. Beyond this, the firs and jack pines begin to crowd the north slopes of the ridges. On the southern and western flanks, there are open bunch-grass slopes lying warm to the sun; while up on the very summit, there stand fine forests of larch and spruce.

With the approach of autumn, a gentle stillness steals over this high country. For weeks, it lies wrapped in the smoky blue haze of fall. Gradually frost and falling temperatures touch the trees. At first there is only the faintest hint of changing colors in the landscape. But as the days grow shorter, the flaming foliage intensifies its impact on the mountains. Before long, they begin to blaze with banners of golden glory.

Along the lake, birches turn from green to yellow to bronze. In the streambeds and damp draws, poplars are dressed with golden radiance. The vine maples and sumac are scarlet. But best of all, the mountain larches glow with golden light.

Of all our western forest trees, the larch is one of my favorites, only because of its autumn splendor. And few are the fall seasons that I fail to spend at least one day walking gently beneath their golden spires in the high country.

Unlike their eastern cousins—the lovely little tamaracks that struggle to survive in the sickly swamps and sloughs that have been left behind the last ice age—the western larch can be a regal mountain monarch. There are larches within ten miles of my doorstep that thrust their great golden crowns two hundred feet into the sky. They stand solid and secure on huge, towering trunks, some of which are four to five feet through at the butt. In spite of their rather thin, fragile, rusty-red bark, some of them have withstood repeated forest fires across the long years of their rugged lives on the ridges.

This past week I set out on my annual pilgrimage to pay honor and respect to these grand giants. The morning light, streaming clear and uncluttered through their feathery foliage, was like fine-spun gold. The trees glowed with an incandescent light, which left the impression they were actually aflame with inner fire. Never had I been so deeply stirred by the living loveliness of the larches. They cloaked the high hills in golden glory. Giant gashes and splashes of vivid yellow ran among the green slopes and rock ridges in bold abandon.

I went to walk softly beneath some of the golden giants. Their glory had been strewn in profusion upon the ground. The forest floor was carpeted with their needles, which were turning bronze and brown.

Suddenly I happened upon an open forest glade in the very depths of a heavily forested draw. Momentarily, I could not believe what I saw. The first overwhelming impression was that I stood in a great cathedral. Several acres of open ground were covered with closely cropped green grass, where range cattle and deer had grazed. A silver stream ran through the meadow, and scattered around it stood gigantic larches, shining gold in the October sunshine.

For a few minutes, I could scarcely move or speak. I simply stood there, awestruck. It was a scene more superb than any man-made park could ever achieve. The open character of the clearing; the spacious openings between the towering columns; the brilliant contrast of the green sward, provided the perfect setting for viewing these mountain monarchs in all their majesty.

Not even the giant Douglas firs of the West Coast, the redwoods of California or the sequoias of the Sierras had touched or moved my spirit so deeply. As I stood silently in the clearing, it came home to me that some sturdy homesteader had once tried to hew out a home for himself in this peaceful paradise. Not a single old log or scrap of forest debris littered the ground. All of it had been cleared and leveled with loving care. Only here and there the forest giants, too large to cut down with an axe, had been left to grow into these great veterans.

One old stump, silver and gray with age, remained. It still bore axe marks, where a pioneer with muscles of steel and a hoping heart had homesteaded a spot for himself in the hills. Across the little stream, a hand-split log had been placed with care, to serve as a footbridge. Clover and grass seed had been sown and had taken root in the virgin soil. But since the time of its planting, it had been grazed only by stray range cattle and wild mountain deer. They kept it neatly clipped, like a park tended by a loving caretaker.

As I walked softly across the green sward, I could hear the gentle gurgle of the little stream. It was suckled by mountain springs a short distance up the draw. A flock of pine siskins swarmed through the tops of the trees, sending down soft shoers of golden needles. This fresh-fallen larch debris dappled the green grass in gay colors, like a plush floor covering.

None of this startling beauty had been expected. It swept over me in momentous wonderment. Few, few indeed, were the human eyes that had ever set sight upon this spot. I was honored to be among the privileged people to set foot here.

It was with genuine reluctance that I finally turned to walk away from that serene spot. There lay upon my soul the inescapable awareness that I had glimpsed a fragment of mountain glory known to but a handful of mortals. Such moments are precious, rare and oftentimes very far apart. They are granted to us by God, as joyous reminders of His own wondrous character and dignity. He deals with us in such ways to make us understand a little of His loving care. His presence surrounds us on every side, yet how slow we are to sense and know: "Father, You are here."

As I came down off the mountain, a deep, upwelling sense of well-being engulfed me. Though it was late October, the sun was warm; its touch tanned my face and browned my bare arms. Not a single stray cloud hovered in the open skies, yet a heavy haze hung in the still autumn air. Distant hills and ridges lay swathed in multihued shades of blue. Those close at hand were almost blue-black, especially where the afternoon shadows slipped across the slopes. The distant ridges lay faint and almost pale, in pastel tones of blue and gray and misty turquoise.

There was a joyous sense of space and serenity to the mountain landscape. This was intensified by the vivid contrast of color that came from the drifts of larch trees running across the slopes. With the late afternoon sun shining through the fragile foliage, it looked like golden filagree. There were royal colors, blue and gold, spread across the landscape in wild and beautiful profusion.

The Master Artist, with deft strokes and delicate touches, had painted upon the canvas of my memory a scene that time would not erase. It was more perfect than any artist's landscape. It pulsed with light and life that had its origin within His own heart and mind.

I came home to "Still Waters" humbled in spirit, happy in heart, replete with bodily rejuvenation. The mountains had enriched me that day, and I was at peace.

Looking south from "Still Waters," across the clear-blue expanse of the lake, one sees the mighty mass of McIntyre Bluff. It is a gigantic rock prominence, sheered off on one side, leaving great vertical cliffs of granite that tower above the valley floor.

Legend has it that in one of the intertribal wars between the local Indians, a band of warriors was driven over the bluff in flight. They plunged to their awful deaths, crushed on the boulders lying at the base of the precipice. Even now, there are those who maintain that the mountain bears the resemblance of a bold Indian chief with prominent nose, protruding cheekbones and jutting jaw.

Geologists insist that the bluff was originally part of a natural glacial barrier that blocked the lower end of the valley. Its mass held back the melting glacial waters that flooded the entire valley into one enormous lake. Eventually, with warming weather and increasing runoff from melted snow on the encircling mountains, the original body of water burst its bounds. In a huge flooding, the initial dam of natural debris and glacial fill was washed away. Behind the flooding, only the gigantic bluff remained, as well as the interconnected chain of beautiful lakes that now adorn the valley.

On the other side of the valley, directly across from the bluff, is a remarkable small canyon. It is cut through solid stone, with sheer, winding walls, by an exquisite, clear-running mountain stream. This rather remarkable cleft in the rocks is called McIntyre Canyon. It is much less spectacular than the gigantic canyons of the southwestern United States, but it is still a spot of unusual vistas and mellow moods.

Access to it can be reached in just a few minutes from "Still Waters." Sometimes I work my way up the canyon from the valley below, or on the other hand explore it from the hills by climbing down through its steep-walled gorge.

The canyon is the sort of place one comes for hours of quiet contemplation and gentle reflection. It is not the sort of spot where chattering companions or noisy, ringing banter is in place.

Somehow, whenever I walk up through this defile, there lies upon my spirit a sense of the endless ages that water has been at work here, wearing away stone. This is no great, rushing river, like the Colorado that carved out the Grand Canyon. Instead it is a very modest mountain stream that tumbles from pool to pool in its laughing course through the hills.

In its passage across the centuries it has carved, chiseled and sculpted the gray stone into fantastic flowing formations. The swirling white water, streaming softly over and around the rocks, smooths and polishes their surfaces, to shining perfection. The grain of granite and veins of quartz that interlace their grayness lie exposed in wondrous beauty beneath the flowing water.

Out of the grim gauntness of the hills, a free-running stream has fashioned a masterpiece of exquisite beauty and splendor.

Sometimes I stand on the damp stone and reflect upon its exquisite character. I am reminded that, in similar manner, only the free flow of the river of God's own Spirit through my hard and stony life fashions it into something of beauty. Only the eternal impact of His presence produces a character of worth and loveliness.

In the stillness of this canyon, ferns and mosses flourish in the damp spots. Despite the dreadful desert heat, down in the deep and shadowed defiles there is coolness and dampness. Spray and mist and the steady evaporation of tumbling water from the stream insure the survival of water-loving plants. Their spores and seeds may have been borne here by birds in flight or by the vagrant mountain winds. No matter how, here they found favorable conditions to start life and establish themselves upon the cracked and weathered surface of the stone.

Throughout its length, the canyon is a shadowed gorge, yet also a natural garden. Besides mosses and lichens, there are banks of bracken, plus gnarled and twisted birches and poplars that have found a foothold in some fissure of the rock. There are beds of wild roses that glow pink in summer and red in fall, when their hips turn scarlet and their foliage flames like fire. There are sturdy firs and patient old ponderosa pines, whose horny roots have forced their strong fingers around the rough rocks, gripping them in a gnarled and viselike grasp. No rushing wind or flooding freshet can ever wrench them from their rocky handholds in the canyon world.

There is music in this canyon, too—wild music, mountain music—music not made by any human enterprise. It is the melodic strains of a stream singing over stone.

It is the muted notes of water murmuring in its gentle flow from pool to pool. It is the gaiety and rhythm of wavelets splashing on rocks, dancing on stage after stage of water-washed stone.

None of this is planned or programmed. It does not come stereotyped. The canyon music rises and falls in intensity with the passing of the seasons. In winter it is hushed and stilled by snow and ice. In spring it rises in tempo with flooding snow melt. In summer it sparkles and scintillates with sunshine. In autumn it is quiet and subdued, freshened by fall showers, but mellow with the blue mood of mountain haze and golden days.

As the hill breezes blow across the canyon country, they carry its song to any who will pause and listen. Sometimes the sound comes strongly, surely, stridently. The tumbling of water and thunder of its fall are trombones and drums sounding in the hills. On other occasions the faint, fine notes of a free-flowing stream are violins, whose high notes sing through the trees and reach for the sky through the narrow cleft above the canyon floor.

There are other notes here, too: the call of the rare canyon wren, who nests in the cliff face; the cry of the slate-gray water ouzel darting from pool to pool; the plaintive song of the song sparrow that echoes from the shadows and sets our spirits singing.

The canyon is a place of many moods and happy hours. It is a spot that reminds man that God, our Father, has been at work on the world a very long time. His work has been good and beautiful and sublime. Nor is it done yet.

Seventeen
Breaking Ground

When looking for a spot to settle, one of the essential attributes it had to possess was a patch of ground suitable for a garden. One of my dreams was to enjoy again the pleasure of producing and harvesting my own fresh, tender, homegrown vegetables.

For a number of years, while busily engaged with other responsibilities, there had not been either time or opportunity to enjoy gardening. Life in apartments and condominiums in a city setting deprives one of this delight. Urban residents may not realize it, but cement walls and asphalt streets have a way of isolating people from the healing impulse of trees and grass, fields and flowers. And in my inner soul there had always lingered

115

the deep, persistent, at times painful longing for a bit of soil: A place where I could plant peas and beans; a spot where my own sun-kissed tomatoes and cucumbers could be plucked, just at their peak of ripened perfection, to provide heaping bowls of crisp, fresh salads.

Happily, "Still Waters" had some open ground, long ago roughly cleared, but never cultivated. The day we decided to buy the property, I had walked carefully over all of its tangled land. Young poplar saplings, wolf willows and mountain alders were springing up in wild abandon everywhere. Their roots ran in every direction, crisscrossing the woodland clearing in unchecked confusion. If left alone, in just a few more summer seasons the place would have reverted to native forest.

One of the first strenuous tasks I tackled was to chop out all this new growth. The piles of young shoots, along with weeds and other invading plants, were gathered up and burned in blazing pyres. There is something very primitive, very elemental, very much of the pioneer instinct in such work. It is intensely satisfying. It takes one back to beginnings. It is an inherent part of the ancient art of taking untamed land and turning it into a homestead; a place where a man decides to sink his roots a spell; a living monument to the end of his wandering days.

During the first summer, I kept the ground clean and clear with a mower. This was not easy. I did not want our tranquil setting disturbed unduly with the screaming sounds of a power mower, so the price to pay for peaceful days was to push an ancient hand mower over the rough ground. A kindly neighbor had freely and spontaneously offered to give me his old reel mower, if I

would just take it away. It was exactly what I needed, not
only to clip the grass short, but also to harden the muscles in my legs, arms and back.

In the early hours just after dawn, while the desert air
was still cool, the ground would be mowed in gentle joy.
The green grass glistened silver under the shining
dampness of its dew. And my face and back glistened
with drops of perspiration forced from the skin by the
exertion of my body. Both the meadow and my muscles
benefited from this morning exercise.

Every time I walked across the sward, I dreamed and
planned just where the garden would grow best. I chose
a corner where the slope of the ground faced south and
west. Here the soil would be warmed to the utmost by
the sun that arched across the valley from range to mountain range. It was a spot, too, with excellent drainage.
Best of all, I knew, from planting some ornamental trees
there in early spring, that its topsoil was deep and dark,
rich with the accumulated humus of uncounted centuries.

But it would not be easy digging.

Again, I was determined to do the labor by hand.

I did not wish the roar of a tractor or tiller to disturb or
desecrate the quiet calm and sensitive stillness of our
Indian-summer days. Their quiet tranquility and still serenity were a special quality, which no modern machine
was allowed to dispel.

It would be a tough task to turn this virgin sod. It had
never been penetrated with the point of a sharp shovel.
Its earth had never been turned to face the sun. No one
had ever stuck a spade in this soil to plant a seed or grow
a crop. In truth, this was to break new ground. And in

that breaking there would be co-mingled sweat and joy.

It was late fall when I began to dig. It was a job that could never be done in a day, a week, ten days or even two weeks. For the better part of a month, my back would bend over this patch of dark earth. The warm autumn sunshine and the heavy labor of my own straining muscles would send little trickles of perspiration trickling across my forehead, face and forearms. Sweat would stand out on my shoulders, back and legs, bared to the blue skies. But it was hearty labor, done with all my heart. It was glad work, done with genuine gaiety. It was sweet toil, deeply satisfying to my spirit.

As my shovel plunged deep into the dark, mellow earth, it would encounter roots and rocks. An antique wheelbarrow, built of solid steel, with its iron wheel and accumulated coat of dried concrete, stood ever beside me. Again and again and again, I piled it high with stones and boulders wrenched from their sockets beneath the sod.

Some stones and rocks were so large and massive I could just barely roll them into the tray of the overturned barrow. Then, shoving and heaving with all my might, the wheelbarrow would be turned upright. Thus I hauled tons and tons of stone from the garden patch. The rocks were used to reinforce and enhance the lake frontage, where the lap of the waves tended to erode away the banks. So in truth I was accomplishing two tasks at once.

As day followed day of digging, the garden plot grew ever larger and more attractive. Black earth, mellow, friable and fertile, lay smooth and silky beneath the sun. It was free, too, of roots and stumps. For with fierce determination, I had torn the tangled mass of underground growth from the soil. The matted roots of snowberry, sumac and wild roses had been heaped in piles. These, too, would add fuel to the last fall fire that cleared the ground ready for spring seeding.

At last, one glorious October morning, the work was done. With enormous pleasure, I stood back to cast my eyes over the garden plot. Already I could see it flourishing with fruits and vegetables the coming summer.

Momentarily I paused and reflected. No doubt it was just as great a job for God, the Good Gardener, to produce His fruits in the little garden of my soul.

Eighteen
Gathering Wood

When we came to "Still Waters," one of our serious intentions was to become as self-sufficient as possible. This was to apply to not only the production of our own fruit and vegetables, but also our fuel requirements.

The little cottage, once it was properly insulated and winterized for cold weather, would be fairly simple to heat. It had only 440 square feet of floor space, every foot of which was used to maximum advantage. With the installation of our wood stove, which served as a combination cook stove, heater and open fireplace, the place could be kept as cosy and warm as a kitten's ear.

With continually escalating energy costs, it made good sense for us to try and supply our own heat from the

wood we could salvage from the lake, as well as the fuel
we could find in the nearby hills. In all of this, there was
a decided degree of fun, excitement and pleasure. It is
much more rewarding to gather one's own wood, with
the expenditure of one's own energy, than merely to pay
some public utility to provide it.

The heat and flames and fragrance from the fuel was
doubly precious because of the little trips and happy
hours outdoors spent in collecting it. As the old saying
goes, cutting one's own wood warms you twice over: first
in the sweat and labor of sawing and splitting, second, in
the gentle radiation of its warmth in the living room.

Often, as I sat and listened to the splintering, crack-
ling sounds of its burning, I was borne back again into
the woods or along the lake, where it had been collected.
On chill, clear, frosty nights, when the stars outside
sparkled against the blackness of the desert darkness,
the lively flames would leap and dance in a similar
shimmering light. The energy of a hundred summer suns
was released and radiated into the room to enliven the
night.

The wood I retrieved from the lake was always somewhat of a surprise. The lake itself was fringed with a
mixed stand of mountain alder, willow, black birch and
poplar. Some of these the beavers felled for food or
material with which to construct their lodges. For one
reason or another, pieces of these "beaver trees," as I
called them, would break away from their original site,
to be washed across the lake by wind and waves.

After almost every heavy blow from the northwest, a
random collection of waterlogged wood was tossed up
on our tiny gravel beach or caught in the tules along the

shore. This bounty of free fuel always tickled my fancy. It was a bit like a fairy tale, to think my wood was being felled by my beaver friends, then ferried across the lake by the wind to be delivered free of charge at the front door.

A few days drying in the heat of our dry desert air, and this wood was ready for the saw and woodpile, where it hardened into first-class fuel. I enjoyed sawing up these slender poles. The physical exertion hardened my muscles and trimmed my body to that of a lithe young athlete.

There were occasional days when good-sized logs would come drifting down the river channel. How they got there was always a bit of a mystery. For a few days they would float around the lake, providing perfect perches for ducks, gulls, terns or crows that loved to alight on them. Eventually, when they came closer to the cottage, I would slip out in the canoe and tow them home for extra firewood. This was always a rather tricky little task, because it was easy to tip the canoe while taking the log in tow.

Other times, I would slip across the lake and find choice pieces of trees and logs that were lodged along the shore, stuck on sandbanks or caught in the bulrushes. These, too, would be loaded in the canoe to be carried home for fuel.

Perhaps even more exciting and pleasurable than these canoe excursions were the days I went to the hills for wood. The *wood days* were chosen with great care. Somehow one had to go in search of winter wood in just the right mood. There was something almost sacramental about it. It was a search for wood suitable to be sacrificed on the flames.

In these quests, I purposely avoided cutting any living, growing, vigorous tree that adorned the woods with its foliage and form. Instead, I deliberately chose to gather what I could from trees or branches or upturned roots that lay upon the ground.

Loggers and fallers long ago had cut and slashed their wasteful way through the rough hills back of us. A tangle of twisted logging tracks and trails traversed the tough terrain. Here there were thousands of stumps to remind a man of the fine forests that had taken untold centuries to clothe these rugged ridges in glorious greenery. Many of the choicest trees were gone; still, sturdy second-generation conifers were taking their place. And in among these latter timber stands, there remained remnants of old, tough trees, which made fine fuel.

Often the prostrate trunks and limbs that still survived the long years of weathering were pieces of wood richly impregnated with saps and resins that prevented rot and decay. The wind-twisted trunks and rough, gnarled limbs turned silver-gray beneath summer sun and winter snow. When put to the flames, their pitchy fibers would burn with fierce heat and flashing flames, to leave behind a bed of glowing coals.

It was like prospecting for precious ore to go in search of such mountain-grown fuel. It was a real find to stumble on some prostrate old veteran, half-buried beneath the accumulated duff of fallen needles, cones and twigs of half a century. Protruding from the forest floor would be the hard, jagged old fir knots or twisted pine limbs that had turned hard as old bone.

Often these were so brittle with age that their wood

could be readily broken by shattering them against a sharp stone. No need, even, for an axe or saw. All that was required to bear home a bountiful supply of beautiful bone-dry wood were sharp eyes, a knowing heart, and arms strong enough to gather up armfuls of the wondrous fuel.

This was conservation at ground level. This material, which otherwise would have wasted away and posed a fire threat to the forests, was used to maximum benefit and joy.

Occasionally I came across trees that had been blown down by the wind or overturned by recent road crews. They would lie not far from the open roads and tracks. Sometimes it would take a little extra work to clear a path to where they lay. Rocks and roots and the debris of broken branches would have to be removed so I could get at this treasure trove.

Last summer, I found a huge vine maple that had been overturned and torn from a creek bed by a caterpillar tractor making a new road. The multitrunked tree had ruthlessly been shoved out of the soil, then pushed aside, to wither away in the summer heat. It was a sad spectacle. Normally vine maples are little more than very sturdy shrubs. Seldom do they exceed twenty feet in height. Their main claim to fame is the gorgeous array of autumn colors that adorn their foliage. Some of these shrubby trees, rooted in the cliffs behind the cottage, carry leaves that vary in color from pale green to vibrant scarlet—all at the same time.

But this uprooted specimen was a huge vine maple. Its main trunk, nearly ten inches in diameter, was the largest I had ever seen in the species. Now it no longer could paint the hills with its fall colors. Like a soldier stricken in battle, it lay fallen and forlorn on the forest floor. Its life was done.

It took the better part of a whole morning to trim away its labyrinth of intertwined limbs, then cut it up into stove-length pieces. When I split up its creamy-white wood, which was tight-grained, I knew I had some of the finest fuel to come out of any forest. Its sawdust was fragrant, and its wood would burn with an intense, clear heat matching the best anthracite coal.

Almost with reverence and genuine tenderness, I took it home. As I stacked the clean, smooth-barked slabs in the sun, I knew I was storing away energy and warmth for many a winter evening. When the winds tore across the lake; shivered the birch branches above our roof and howled around the house, the vine maple would make up for it all with its fierce, enduring flames, which would leap up the chimney, driving back the blizzard's chill.

Nineteen
Swans in the Mist

There is a beautiful mountain river that cascades over a gnarled rock ridge several miles upstream from our lake. Its cold, clear waters rush and rumble through the broken gap cut in the stone by centuries of tumbling water. The shining spray and roaring white rapids are in vivid contrast to the blue stillness of the lake beyond and the sky above.

Farther down, its channel has been constricted by the industry of man. Its wild, native turbulence has been tamed. It runs softly, in still, smooth stretches between lush green fields of hay and grain. Here cattle graze quietly on the verdant meadows, their sleek red hides reflecting the warm sunlight like shimmering silk. It is a

placid and pleasant setting, enhanced by the high hills
and bold bluffs of brown rock that march down the flanks
of the river's valley.

Gradually the ranchlands are replaced by marshlands.
Here the river spreads itself into swampy mud flats,
where bulrushes, blackbirds, herons, and a host of other
marsh birds abound. This is where the Canada geese
come with their fledglings in the spring. It is where the
thump of the bittern and the shrill cries of the grebes
echo across the tule beds. These are the ancient calls of
the wild, which have been a part of this lake for ten
thousand years.

In fall a peculiar phenomenon occurs over these reed
beds and river mouth at dawn each day. Ghostlike
plumes of snow-white mist begin to billow up above the
surface of the stream. They are not stationary or still.
Instead, the rising mists, like wild white horses rearing
up in ranks of gleaming white, go galloping across the far
side of the lake.

The clouds of phantom chargers are borne along
strongly by the down drafts of cool air coming off the
high country. Manes tossing in the morning light, they
sweep out across the lake, then lose themselves in the
warmth and sunlight of the dry, desert air.

Into the white mists fly all sorts of birds, most of them
winged visitors heading south. They come in hundreds,
dark bodies bursting through the whiteness as they wing
in from the north to rest briefly on the lake. Sometimes
they simply vanish from view as the clouds of vapor engulf them. But through its white shrouds come their contented calls, as they feed eagerly on the rich weed beds.

Occasionally one or several pair of wild trumpeter

swans come in to land on the lake. Of all our feathered friends, they are the most noble and regal. Their graceful forms and immaculate white plumage grace the blue waters in resplendent contrast. In ancient times, the trumpeters were reported to have nested in these marshes. But the advent of modern machinery and the cacophony of modern men gradually discouraged the shy birds from remaining on their traditional grounds. So at best they are here only a few short weeks in late fall.

The other morning I watched a pair wheel proudly over the lake. Even their flight was grand and stately. They moved in wondrous unison, like a pair of superb ballet dancers in a sublime *pas de deux*. Unhurried, unruffled—smoothly sailing across the stage of blue water, blue sky, brown hills and bronze reed beds—they soared effortlessly, sheathed in shining iridescence, their outstretched wings reflecting sunlight.

No ballet performance ever impressed me more. Their consummate natural artistry and gentle grace surpassed the loftiest passages from Tchaikovsky's *Swan Lake*.

With majestic beauty, they circled down into the mist, their flowing forms gradually melding into the enveloping whiteness. It was as if they had vanished into vapor, passing silently yet serenely from life into death.

It was a poignant pageantry. It had lasted but a few fleeting moments. It had been observed only by one man. But, as with so many of God's great gifts, the man was richer for having gladly received it.

Twenty
Before Daybreak

At four in the morning, on a clear, moonlit November night, the desert air can be crystal bright. The whole world lies sharp, still, etched with silver light. The stars pulse with intensity. The moon moves majestically across the night sky, appearing to drop steadily toward the western ridges. There is an awesome, wondrous breathlessness to the valley.

These are those still, sacred, special hours, in which the spirit of a man is moved upon by the Spirit of God. It was under desert skies like this that many of the divine revelations have come to the seers and prophets of all ages.

Only a random stray leaf, left here and there, hangs

unmoving amid the delicate fretwork of the bare tree branches. Their lacelike intertwined twigs form a fragile pattern of black filagree against the mellow moonlight. Nothing stirs. Not a leaf trembles. Not a branch bends. Not a wavelet moves on the lake. Momentarily, the whole earth appears to be cast in priceless pewter.

There is an overpowering sensation of stillness: a quiet so acute that any sound of a passing vehicle would be an insolent intrusion. The drone of a distant plane would be a desecration. The clatter of man's clamorous civilization would be an imposition of discordant notes out of harmony with the spheres in space.

These quiet, morning moments are precious points in one man's brief life. Yet they are the essence of the eternal; for out of the endless, timeless immensity of eternity, God speaks softly, clearly and specifically to the waiting soul: "Be still and know that I am God." The words are poignant and appropriate. His own gracious Spirit is present, to commune with the heart quietly humbled by the breathless beauty about him. In such interludes, my soul is stilled, my spirit is at rest. All is well.

Amid the ebb and flow of the shifting tides of human history, these eternal values remain. No one can rob me of the stars. No man can deprive me of the moon's majestic mood. No crisis of civilization can completely eclipse the stillness of the desert night. These remain and endure. They are beyond the grasp of rapacious men, yet they are freely available to the most humble heart, which briefly but sincerely is open and responsive.

I have often sat alone beneath the stars and moon, wrapped in the wonder of their enchantment. Their soft and silver splendor spread across the earth is free for the taking. It is lavished with love across the landscape. It is spread with exquisite artistry upon rocks and grass, upon trees and water. Everywhere one turns, the light of the night glows gently. It makes the earth a magic sphere, suspended in space, shining with reflected light that may have taken ten thousand years to reach it from remote stars in the depths of distant space.

I cannot, with my finite mind and limited human perception, comprehend the enormity of eternity. Nor can I reach out to embrace the uncounted, unknown millions of stars, suns and galaxies of the universe. But I can bow my soul before the beauty of dawn, breaking now across the eastern ranges, and whisper softly, "Oh God, my Father, You are here; You are near; and You are very dear."

Inherently, in the fragile loveliness of this chill November morning, there is also present enormous integrity. For untold centuries, for millenia of unnumbered seasons, the steady rhythm of sun and moon, stars and planets has swung serenely across the skies. Men— simple men and wise men—have looked and longed and marveled at such majesty.

Man's puny pride, his arrogant intellect, his brazen bravado, have had no part in planning or programming this pageantry. It is strictly a divine production. Only God Himself could arrange such grandeur. It pulverizes petty pride.

For this I am glad.

It reassures me: *"Thou, God,* changest not!"

All else may.

Twenty-One
November Morning

November can be bleak and bare and bitterly cold. But it can also be hauntingly beautiful in its melancholy muted tones, saddened by the last tattered leaves tumbling from the trees; the last forlorn flights of waterfowl leaving the icebound lakes; the last glimpses of gray ground, frozen like cast iron, waiting to be cloaked in winter white.

This was one of those mornings.

When I crawled out from beneath the warm wool comforter of the bed, I could feel a distinct bite in the air. There was a sharpness to its edge. I looked out across the lake, whose edges shone silver with a skim of fresh ice.

If I was to make one last canoe trip across the lake

before final freeze-up, it would have to be now. A gigantic breakfast of cereal, toast, bacon and eggs, whose delicious fragrance filled the cottage, fortified me for the venture.

Taking my paddles, binoculars and axe, along with wool jacket, cap and gloves, I launched the canoe in our little sandy cove. The thin glaze of transparent ice crackled and splintered around the sleek green hull as I pushed off from the beach, breaking out into open water beyond.

Scarcely had I gotten out into the lake when a gusty wind came up. In just a few moments, it was moving the icy water in rolling waves. Its frosty edge cut my exposed face, making me set my jaw and grit my teeth in grim defiance of the worst it could do.

Fiercely, I dug the paddle into the stormy waters. I doggedly fought the wind that threatened to capsize the frail little craft, so fragile and easily flung about. My muscles had been hardened and honed by the summer's heavy work. Moving rocks, planting trees, mowing grass, digging virgin sod, splitting wood and mixing concrete had stripped away the softness and left me tough and trim.

Persistently, powerfully, patiently I plowed across the lake. No November blow would hold me back from making the opposite shore. The icy water splashed against the prow. It slapped against the sides. It went swishing angrily beneath the thin belly of the canoe as I drove it against the wind. At last we came into the more quiet waters that lay in the lee of a long wooded point. There I could reduce the rate of my strokes and rest the paddle occasionally.

A last pair of belated mallards sprang up from the lake

behind a clump of bulrushes, where they had been shel-
tering. Their explosion sent a spray of silver droplets
shining into the sun, which was just lifting over the high
hills. Necks outstretched, bodies straining with rapid
upward wing beats, the two big birds climbed boldly
above me. Suddenly they circled and sped down the
valley, headed south for sunshine and warmer days. At
that instant, I wished fervently that I too possessed the
incredible freedom of uninhibited flight.

Gently the canoe edged its way along the sheltered
shore. I finally found a small patch of sand on a bank
beneath some aged black birch. Here I put its bow up on
the shore, feeling glad to have found such a pleasant
landing. Pulling it up well onto the sand, safe from wind
and waves, I headed into the hills.

To my surprise, the wind gained in velocity. Angrily it
gusted and howled around the giant walls of rock that
towered above the lake. As they faced south, I had as-
sumed they would be somewhat sheltered from the
northern storms. Instead, the rushing air twisted and
turned through the valley, bending the trees with its
might, following the contour of the land like a hound hot
on a trail.

Today there would be little relief anywhere from its
onslaught. It gathered up the bleached, brown bundles
of ripened knapweed and tumbleweed, tossing them
across the benches, rolling them down the banks, scat-
tering their sturdy seeds in every direction.

A stray raven, like a black bandit, also tumbled in the
wind. His raucous cry swept along with him as he
flapped through the forest and sought more-sheltered
terrain.

I hugged the foot of the high cliffs, hoping to find a

sun-warmed spot between the gray boulders that frost had forced off the mountain face. Steadily I worked my way up into higher ground. My exertions made the warm air from my heaving lungs come out in white plumes that quickly vanished in the cold air. But the stiff climb kept me warm until I suddenly broke out into a little sheltered basin where all was still. Here there was a virtual sun trap, where the feeble November sun warmed the stone and tempered the air.

There was a sweet sensation of repose here. I pushed back my heavy wool cap and let the sun's rays caress my face. I pulled off my lined gloves and felt its feeble warmth on my gnarled and sun-browned hands. Here was stillness amid the storm, serenity amid severity. The contrast made it doubly precious.

Life is often like that. How little would most of us genuinely appreciate our Father's gracious gifts, were it not for the adversity of life's storms.

I had luxuriated in this gentle spot only a few moments when my ears detected the persistent, piping call of a canyon wren. The tiny brown bird, with its snowy-white bosom, flitted across the rock face above me. Erratically, he flew from crevasse to crevasse in the cliff, searching for insects with his long probing beak. Never for an instant did he relent in his chirping.

Much to my delight, he began to approach me. I stood as still as stone. Hugging the rocks, I endeavored to be as unmoving and inconspicuous as possible. Almost before I knew it, he was flitting over the rocks less than six feet from my face. It was my closest encounter with this beautiful and rather rare wren. He did not linger long in my company. Satisfied that he had searched the rocks around me well enough, he flew up the mountain, leaving me glad that I had come that morning, in spite of the weather.

Slowly I worked my way back through the forest. It was a comfort to tread softly on the deer trails beneath the big, red-barked ponderosa pines. Their long needles on the forest floor provided a cushioned path for my heavy hiking boots. Tramping woodland trails in silence has always been a balm to my wild and restless spirit. It does something to restore and refresh a man who quickly wearies of city streets and the noisy clangor of man's metropolitan world. The rush and confusion and tensions of the twentieth century strain us more than we know. For taut minds and tired nerves, a few miles of forest paths are a wondrous panacea.

I came across a gorgeous cluster of a dozen young junipers. They were growing vigorously in the shelter of a giant, dead fir. I marked the spot well in my memory, promising myself to return one spring day to dig one up for planting at "Still Waters." There its fine, feathery foliage would adorn one of the rockeries and gladden our hearts every time we looked out over the lake. It would be an enduring reminder of this November day.

Back at the canoe, I decided to load it with some of the sun-dried, bone-hard limbs of black birch that lay in profusion beneath the trees. The wood lying in the bottom of the frail craft would give greater stability in the choppy waters on my way home. Happily, the wind would be to my back, so it would be a swift crossing.

Out on the lake once more, the canoe sprang to life under the driving impulse of my powerful strokes. It literally surged ahead on each succeeding wave that the wind drove beneath it, like a charger champing on the bit. With the wind against my back and the sun on my face, we skimmed homeward toward the cottage in high spirits.

During the morning the wave action had fragmented the ice along the shore and in the tule beds. As we neared the beach, the sound of ten thousand tinkling ice bells rang through the chill, clear air. Fractured, broken, glasslike ice particles tinkled against one another and against the globes of ice that encircled each bulrush stem. Bending and blowing in the wind, they produced a symphony of sound delicately blending the innumerable sounds of a thousand ice bells in the breeze.

It was an exquisite homecoming. November was not all drab and bad. This had been a morning I would never forget, fashioned in exquisite beauty from wind and water, forest and frost.

Twenty-Two
Hike in the Hills

One of the great attractions of our gentle life at "Still Waters" consists of frequent hikes in the nearby hills. Few people are so fortunate that, within ten minutes of stepping out their front door, they can be in wild and untamed terrain. In our case, this high, broken country—with its sagebrush benches, giant broken-rock cliffs, open parklike forests and rugged hills—is ideal for hiking.

Part of its great magnetism also lies in the rich array of wildlife that is native to the area, both animals and birds. There is, as well, a wide diversity of trees, shrubs, grasses and flowers that lends interest to any ramble up the rock ridges. And, naturally, the broken character of

141

the landscape, with its lakes and streams, provides wondrous long views of breathtaking beauty.

Any time that I set out on foot, a sandwich in my pocket and binoculars slung over my shoulder, it is with a keen sense of excitement and adventure. No two trips are ever the same, and it is surprising what new vignettes of wildlife or natural wonder will enliven my mountain rambles.

One autumn hike I took still lingers with limpid clarity in my memory. Most of the final tasks around the cottage had been cleared away. The garden was spaded and lay waiting for winter weather. The woodpile was piled high. All the trees were trimmed. The beach had been cleared and was freshly sanded. The road was graveled with crushed red shale from the hills. So all was well. There were free days now, to roam happily in the autumn sunshine.

I set out with a friend to climb the cliffs back of our bungalow. We had not hiked more than 400 yards when I spotted a select band of bighorn sheep. I say select, because among them were several superb rams. One of these was a monster—a big black male of magnificent proportions. Proudly he carried a commanding set of horns that were approaching full curl. Many a hunter would risk life and limb for such a trophy.

It surprised me to see such a splendid specimen so close to my cottage. How he had managed to elude the sportsmen for so many seasons was somewhat of a miracle, for every fall, these hills were hunted hard by hunters in quest of outstanding rams.

To my unbounded delight, the big black ram did not bolt. Instead, he sensed that the hunting season was over and he need fear no hurt from me. In any case, he was so intent on the ewes in his band that he scarcely gave us any notice.

It was a moving spectacle, to watch this superb specimen of his species move across the broken terrain with such proud and regal might. The easy, powerful, fluid strength of his enormous muscles rippled beneath his shining coat. Every step he took bespoke his majestic prowess. With exultant grace he would bound up and up, from boulder to boulder in great steel-spring leaps that looked so easy. Yet a man scrambling over that same ground would have to stretch and strain and struggle to even start to cross the rocky chasms.

With giant leaps, he would launch himself from ledge to ledge. Where I would hesitate to even look down because of the yawning chasms below, he would leap across lightly from toehold to toehold, his hooves finding sure footing in the tiniest irregularities of rock or unevenness of stone surface.

The quiet composure of the mighty ram; the calmness of his great yellow eyes; the obvious command of his presence; the sureness of his own superb strength, were all expressions of his wilderness realm. He was a pristine product of a tough and hardy species that had survived in this mountain terrain for uncounted centuries.

The enormous hazards of winter blizzards, raging forest fires, the predation of coyotes, cougars and bears, had been endured and overcome. The relentless pressures from hunters, disease and the inroads of ranchers' cattle on the bighorn range had been met and mastered. In spite of the worst that modern civilization, its men and machinery had done to this mountain realm, the great ram stood there as a symbol of wild majesty.

The sight made my blood race in my veins. It quick-
ened and stirred my spirit. My heart pounded with
primitive pleasure, and I confess that a choking lump
began to rise in my throat.

This was more, much more than mere sentiment. It
was an expression of profound and personal gratitude to
God for the great privilege of having played a small part
in the survival of these wild sheep.

Years and years ago, I had sensed that with increased
development of this valley, the sheep range would be
imperiled. This especially applied to the lower levels
along the lakes, where they came for winter feed. Here
the snow was less deep. Grass and shrubs on the
lakeside benches, swept clear by winter winds, insured
their survival.

Yet, as so often happens, no one in government
seemed to share my personal concern. Homes began to
be built along the lake. Campgrounds, orchards and
roads began to occupy the grassy ground. Fences were
erected, and steadily but surely the wild-sheep range
was being constricted into an ever-diminishing size.

My apprehension was shared with other local wildlife
lovers. A sufficiently aroused number of people banded
together to form a local park-and-wildlife-preservation
society. From time to time, I was invited to come and
address this group. Some of the sessions were thrown
open to the public. So it was that private contributions
were collected to establish a fund, out of which land
could be bought to increase the sanctity of the sheep
range. Bit by bit, wild acreage was purchased, and the
sheep were provided with adequate areas in which they

could graze throughout the severe winter weather.

Little did I dream, in those far-off days, that it would later be my good fortune to have a home in the very heart of this sheep terrain. Little did I think that some of my happiest hikes would be across the hills I had helped to preserve for my wild friends of hoof, wing and claw. Little did I ever envisage the day when, with pounding heart and racing pulse, I would stand in silent wonderment, watching a superb ram standing on the skyline as a salute to my own service to him.

It is of such stuff that dreams and life's richest moments are made. There is a jewellike quality to such interludes. There comes a dazzling, shining, winsome awareness of having had a small share in an enterprise of enduring quality. I call it, in layman's language, having a part in our Father's majestic plans and purposes for the planet.

The bighorn ram, grand and regal in his demeanor that day, was not the only reward that came to my spirit. As I climbed higher along the cliff face, a gorgeous golden eagle sailed past me on outstretched wings, the wind of his passing whistling softly through his stiff flight feathers. He was coursing the cliffs and tumbled rock piles at their base for some sign of rabbits or marmots that might provide a meal. In a matter of moments, the great bird had come and gone, but I was richer for his passing.

As the sun began to drop down toward the blue ridges to the west, I turned toward home. The day would die quickly. Its hours had passed swiftly in the gentle company of my companion.

Striding down through the sagebrush and greasewood, I was suddenly startled by the unexpected explosion of a coyote from his bed beneath a bush. Evidently he had been sound asleep in his snug shelter when I burst in upon him. Crafty creature that he is, this coyote seemed to literally start out of his sleep running full speed, without having to become wide awake. In seconds he had zigzagged through the greasewood, put a rock ridge between himself and us, then melted from sight into the surrounding terrain. I was sure he was the same fellow who sometimes left his telltale tracks across my driveway.

In the gathering dusk we came across a covey of wild and noisy chukar partridges. Swiftly they scattered through the rocks and brush, calling to one another. Often I had thrilled to the haunting sounds of their cries from the cliffs. They were always a reminder that a bit of the wilds will survive and thrive, if given half a chance by man.

Trudging home, tired in muscle and tendon, my spirit was singing and gay. It had been a good day—a great day—a day to be remembered for its joy and splendor in the hills.

Twenty-Three
Neighbors

No man, if he wishes to be a truly joyous person, can live as an island of isolation. Even those of us who are by instinct independent individualists, need neighbors and friends and kin to fully round out our lives. It is a poor person indeed whose days are not enriched by an interchange of love and kindness with his fellow human beings.

All of my life, it has been my wonderful good fortune to experience the warmth, affection and acceptance of good and kindly people. This is one of God's great gifts to me. It matters not where life's adventures have led; always there have been dear, bighearted, generous souls who took me into their circle of friendship.

147

This has been true whether my neighbors were tough-and-hardy ranchers and loggers; whether they were West Coast fishermen or native Indians; whether they were sophisticated scientists, bright intellectuals from the academic world; or whether they were the notorious Masai of the African plains. No matter what status or station a person's background may have been, always it has been possible to find those through whom the milk of human kindness, and God's own gracious love, flowed in full measure to enrich my own life.

When we moved to "Still Waters," I knew this would happen again, and it did. We were treated with a courtesy and kindness that touched me deeply. In fact, the interest, concern and genuine love shown by our neighbors remains as one of the bright, scintillating chapters of our experience there.

Harv was one of the men who helped us get started. He is one of those quiet, strong, gentle people who is ever ready and willing to lend a helping hand. Harv came down and built the cupboards in the cottage. Amid the pungent aroma of cedar sawdust, he sawed and shaped and fitted the fragrant lumber into beautiful built-in fixtures, where we could store clothes and books and boots and bedding.

He is a tall, strong, rawboned man, with a gentle smile and delightful sense of humor. Harv and I manage to take several tramps in the hills together every year. He loves the high country and wild places as fiercely as I do. All of our adventures together are replete with good cheer and lighthearted gaiety. Sometimes we go out to gather great loads of firewood in his big, battered truck. Never have I known a man who can ease a truck over such tough and impossible terrain as well as he can. He seems to literally love his vehicle up the most impossible places. And even though it is a machine built of nuts and bolts, steel and iron, it responds to his touch like a living being.

Harv is the one who came and helped me clear the site for my new toolshed. He can perform more work with a shovel in his big hands than any man I ever met. Rocks and boulders and roots were torn from the ground in short order under his tough hands; hands that can also tune an engine to run sweetly and serenely. He is a top mechanic, who can make iron and metal move when most of us would stand mocked by its malfunction.

Harv's dainty wife, Marie, is almost as tiny as he is tall. She is a vivacious, bubbling, enthusiastic soul. Her culinary skills are special. Any invitation to her home is a treat to superb cooking. Often she has shared her special pickles, preserves and meat with us.

In her kindness and thoughtfulness, she often offers Cheri rides to and from town. And when the two of them are together, I am reminded of a couple of happy schoolgirls away on some hilarious lark together.

Bill was a total stranger to us when we moved to "Still Waters." He and his wife Phyl owned the land adjoining ours. Both of them are people with a profound love for plants and trees and shrubs and flowers. Anything that grows also glows in their care. They have an innate instinct for making things grow. Their lot next to ours, though vacant and unoccupied, resembles a fine English park. Its elegant trees, its borders of beautiful evergreens, its flaming sumac and forsythia, are a never-ending source of pleasure to us.

At his own home, Bill has created a paradise of beauty
out of a barren sagebrush gully. It is now considered one
of the most delightful properties in the whole valley. He
is a specialist in pruning and grafting and budding. His
special hobby is collecting varieties of apple trees. Of
these, he has some 132 sorts growing on his land. Roses
are also his love. At one time, over 1,000 rosebushes
graced his grounds. His big brown hands caress everything that grows in his soil.

Bill installed a new watering system on his lot next
door. In bighearted generosity and thoughtfulness, he
voluntarily offered to run a line to my lot, as well. He felt
it would help to water the new garden I had dug and
spaded with so much sweat and toil. It was a gracious
gesture, a mark of a kindly neighbor.

Seldom did Bill ever come past our place without
stopping in for a few moments of friendly conversation.
Almost always he brought bags or baskets of fruits and
vegetables from his own flourishing fields. Tomatoes,
corn, peppers, peaches, potatoes and even peas that had
been picked on his place, were left on the step at our
front door. Each gift was a token of this dear fellow's
friendly spirit, reaching out to warm our own.

Then there was Richard. He came to our country from
the heart of Old London Town. Like so many En-
glishmen, Dick brought with him a sense of humor, wit,
and good cheer that nothing can suppress.

When first I met Dick, he was a bit of a skeptic. But all
of that has been changed, as the love of God spread
gently into his spirit. Dick has become a buoyant human
being, filled and energized with irrepressible fun. He is
a plumber, ever ready to repair a faulty water line or

install a fixture that would flood out the rest of us.

Out of his own free will, Dick came down to make sure all the old, dilapidated pipes in our place would work at least half-decently. He crawled into the dark and dusty spaces where spiders spun their webs. He turned and twisted his agile frame into awkward corners under sinks and cupboards to couple pipes. Yet, all the time, there flowed from this fellow nothing but good cheer to enliven our days with his delightful wit.

When Cheri was ill, he and Cecile, his joyful wife, would pop in to bring gifts of baking and their own unique brand of get-well good humor. Even the most distraught patient could not help but chuckle with them. And, after all, laughter is the best medicine in all the world. When they left, there remained behind a legacy of love and warm affection.

Just down the road a wee way lived Tom. He was a spry man who, though well into his seventies, still built his own house, cut and split all his own wood, and dug his own garden.

Tom would loan me his truck whenever I needed this sort of transportation. He was glad to store certain precious boxes of films and slides in his cool basement. He was always glad to give any advice I sought that the long years of his own experience had bestowed upon him.

One of my own great and special joys was to attend a service at the little church where Tom worshiped. One morning this courageous, simple layman took the entire service for his fellow parishioners. He spoke happily, boldly, gladly of the great joy and fulfillment that Christ had brought into his life. When we walked out of that little chapel on the hill, I knew that our Father had been there, too, with a smile on His face.

Tom's vivacious wife, Vivian, often drops in with a bowl of strawberries, a bouquet of roses or several of the magnificent Spanish onions that she knows are my special favorite. Tom grows these to perfection on his little plot by the lake. They are sweet and delicious to the palate.

Olga and Carlyle are next-door neighbors: in fact, the only people whose house is adjacent to ours. Olga especially loves the soil, with the reverend intensity of one who realizes that it is upon the earth that all of us depend for our sustenance.

Olga digs and spades and plants and weeds and waters from dawn to dusk. The rattle of her shovel and the sound of her hoe at work on the stony ground of her garden are a constant reminder of her love of the land. She is burned brown as an oak plank with the desert sun. Her strong body and bright eyes are alive with vigor.

Often she slips over to "Still Waters" with cantaloupes, apricots, raspberries or vegetables. She always comes with good cheer. She, too, is full of fun, and we tease each other about the handsome house she and Carlyle are building. Carlyle has spared no pains to make it a fine home, built from concrete, giant bolted beams and great piles of lumber.

Another dear couple who live nearby are Abe and Helen. They have been friends for years, but now they are neighbors. They are sturdy, tough, kindhearted souls, whose industry and diligence have brought them nationwide recognition for their art in taxidermy.

Abe's work is well known from coast to coast on this continent. The birds and animals and hides and horns mounted in their shop grace the homes of outdoorsmen all over North America. But Abe is much more than just a taxidermist; he is also an ardent outdoorsman, and we have shared happy hours in the hills.

His workmanship can be seen everywhere in our little cottage. The exquisite quail lamp on my desk; the handsome elk-horn table in our front room; the mounted meadowlark on the wall; the gorgeous Grant's gazelle hide that Helen trimmed, are all reminders of this couple.

Last fall I asked Abe to make me a small ceiling chandelier from two pair of deer horns. He made a masterpiece of unusual beauty that hangs from our open-beamed ceiling. Like everything he does, it has upon it the mark of a master craftsman.

Abe has shown me where to get shale in the hills for my driveway. He has hauled loads of earth down to our place for building up the rockeries. He has helped me trim the trees that grow so profusely by the lake. He has been a generous, kind and caring friend.

All of these, and others, are people who, in their own individual ways, have injected an element of gaiety, adventure, warmth and enrichment into our lives. We are richer for them. In sincerity and honesty, we give thanks for all of them.

Twenty-Four
Flowers

Flowers have always been a special joy to me. This began with my earliest boyhood. With enormous enthusiasm and industry, my parents developed a gorgeous, parklike place for their home on what had been a barren, broken, rocky hilltop in the heart of Africa.

Our house literally stood in a gigantic garden of glowing color. Every sort of flower seemed to flourish and thrive under my parents' loving touch. Masses of bougainvillea and golden shower cascaded over the roof and porches of our home. Roses, cannas and iris of a hundred hues glowed in the garden. And in the house itself, almost every room was embellished with beautiful arrangements of cut flowers.

Because of this, no matter where life's travels have taken me ever since, flowers have attracted and drawn me strongly. It mattered not whether they were wild blossoms blowing in the breeze on some wild mountain meadow, or whether they were twelve perfect roses that came from a city florist.

The texture, fragrance, color and gaiety of flowers all hold a unique fascination. In the hills, in our home, or in my wife's beautiful blonde hair, they have always been a source of delight and joy.

Around "Still Waters," most of the terrain is tough, sunburned, desert benchland. Yet here wild flowers thrive and blossom in abundance. There are plants as formidable and hardy as greasewood, rabbit brush and spiny cactus. Each flowers in yellow profusion. Mock orange bushes thrive in the rocky draws and spread their delicious fragrance on the desert air. Entire hillsides are radiant with the gold of balsam root.

Some of the flowering plants are very tiny and fragile. The delicate rock rose, the scarlet bugler and wild phlox grow amid the tough bunch grass, gladdening the eye with their brilliance.

Thistles of various sorts thrive here. Their showy flowers, abundant in nectar, provide a bouquet for bees and other insects that are drawn by their brilliance. From late February to mid-October, there is a steady succession of plants and shrubs lending their color to our valley world.

When we moved to "Still Waters," there were no flowers planted there to grace the grounds. The former owners had used skill in landscaping the property, but all of their plantings had been trees and ornamental shrubs. In themselves, these were singularly attractive, but I missed the brightness and cheer of color that flowers bring to any garden.

The first bush I planted was a handsome rhododendron. It was set right beside the lake, in the cool, broken shadows of the birch trees. It flourished in its newfound spot and glowed scarlet in early summer with its handsome red blooms.

A kind friend gave me a healthy plant of ragged robin. This was set in a sunny spot that would make it conspicuous for the hummingbirds. Before the season was over, the little winged acrobats would hover over its fragrant blooms, fighting fiercely for its sweet, pungent nectar.

We were also given a fine specimen of desert evening primrose. This showy plant provided endless interest, both to us and friends who came to visit. Every evening, just as the sun sank behind the western hills, two or three of its huge buds would begin to open. These buds were about the size of my smallest finger. Each was wrapped tightly in a sheath formed by the calyx. Almost as if in slow motion on a screen, each would begin to burst open before our eyes. In about three minutes, the full-bloom petals would unfurl as the calyx leaped open. Then, in striking beauty, the great golden flowers would be fully formed, thrust wide open, waiting for the night moths.

Children, especially, were amazed and excited by this evening performance. They would wait eagerly for the event. And if, perchance, they were fortunate enough to see the giant hummingbird moths come to feed on the flowers, their ecstasy knew no bounds. Gasps of delight and muffled shouts of enthusiasm would burst out in suppressed astonishment.

These showy flowers lasted only one night. When the hot morning sun of the folowing day touched their petals, they faded and wilted. Only a single night were they available to be pollinated by the gray moths. These, with their acute sensors, would detect the primrose nectar on the night air. From afar, often more than a mile across the lake, they would come winging in, to do their crucial work in sustaining the species.

This intricate interaction of plants and insects was a ceaseless reminder to us of the wondrous interrelationship of the natural world around us. This interplay of diverse living organisms that were interdependent for survival and the perpetuation of the species was not something planned or programmed by the ingenuity of man or human intellect.

It might very well be asked which came first, the golden evening primrose or the great gray moth? Each contributed to the survival of the other. Each had its part in preserving the other. Each assured the other of the remarkable perpetuation of its kind.

Sometimes, in the face of such phenomena, my own spirit is stilled and silent. Here I stand in the presence of a phenomenon too complex and intricate and wondrous in design to be shrugged off with a toss of the shoulder. All of this is a remarkable part of my Father's world, arranged and programmed by Him with meticulous precision and beautiful harmony of design.

Besides the flowers that grew wild in the hills around us, many of which I often gathered and bore home for our own bouquets, there were those flowers brought to us by friends and neighbors.

Some of these dear people had beautiful gardens. From their profusion they plucked armfuls of roses, carnations, iris and lillies that were shared with us.

Audrey and Phyllis and Olga and Vivian and Cecile and Connie all came to our little cottage by the lake with arms full of fragrant flowers. There is something very special about receiving flowers from a friend. There is, bound up in the bouquet, much more than so many buds and blooms.

In those flowers is a sharing of beauty. There is a giving of one's own affection and love and warmth. There is an expression of kindness and caring. It is as if to say, in language no human words can fully express, "I'm fond of you. I care deeply about you. I wish to cheer your days. I want to brighten your home. I really love you."

The fragrance, the beauty, the aura of the flowers, speak eloquently of the character and person of the donor. Just knowing and loving such people enriches our souls. And that has been the whole story of our life at "Still Waters."